Against the Tide

Against the Tide
How the top investors beat the markets

Sunil Jagtiani & Richard Lander

A Citywire Publication

First published in Great Britain in 2003 by:
Citywire Financial Publishers Ltd,
1st Floor, 87 Vauxhall Walk, London SE11 5HJ.

ISBN 0-9546559-0-7

INVESTMENT NOTICE
Information provided in Against the Tide is for your general information
and use. In particular, the information does not constitute any form of specific advice or recommendation by Citywire Financial Publishers Ltd. and
is not intended to be relied upon by users in making (or refraining from
making) any investment decisions. Appropriate independent advice should
be obtained before making any such decision.
Citywire Financial Publishers Ltd. is regulated by the Financial Services
Authority.

Authors: Sunil Jagtiani and Richard Lander

Executive Chairman: Lawrence Lever
Chief Executive : David Turner
Publishing Director: George Ball
Project Co-ordinator: Marion Hasson
Editor in Chief: Gavin Lumsden
Investment Funds Editor: David Smith

Designed by Scratch Design (ag@scratchdesign.com)
Printed by Biddles Ltd, Guildford

Contents

Contents

Foreword

Oh to know the secret of consistently successful investing.

If it were a scientific process then it would have been bottled and mass-produced, by now.

But many millions of people invest in active funds run by managers who lay claim to the ability to beat the stockmarket. The fate of these investors' hard-earned cash depends to a great degree on the skill of individual fund managers.

Unfortunately, highly skilled fund managers are few and far between. Most professional investors are swamped by the ebb and flow of the stockmarket, while only a small minority can break free of the tide

This handful of fund managers, through judgement, psychological make up, skill, nerve, or the wisdom of experience, have conquered the markets to the great benefit of investors in their funds. They are more than mere opportunists, able to exploit temporary market inefficiencies which eventually get ironed out by others following hard on their heels. These people have something which is not that easy to imitate or apply.

Sunil Jagtiani, Citywire's funds writer supremo and Richard Lander, our Editorial Director, have conducted searching interviews with a dozen of these top investors, probing in depth how they operate. *Against The Tide* takes in a wide range of investing styles in twelve crisp chapters, deliberately written to be accessible to both investment advisers and their clients. You cannot, after reading this book, go out and become the next Bill Miller or Anthony Bolton, but you can glean valuable insight, which may inform your own investment style or that of your clients. If so we will have achieved what we set out to do - to bring genuine investment expertise to a broader audience so that others can be encouraged in their endeavours to swim successfully 'against the tide'.

I guarantee you a stimulating, thought provoking, read.

Lawrence Lever
Executive Chairman, Citywire Financial Publishers

Introduction

Not so long ago, a male British fund manager charged with fraud appeared in court wearing make-up, a red dress and black high heels. The man in question, a six-foot-tall graduate of Oxford University, called himself 'Beth', short for 'Elizabeth'. Beth, née Peter Young, was the architect of one of the mutual fund industry's biggest scandals. The stellar performance of his award-winning European Fund turned out to be built on a web of front companies which he secretly controlled. Details of the intricate swindle first emerged in 1996, plunging thousands of the small investors affected into great uncertainty. They eventually achieved redress through compensation payments which cost some £400 million. Young was sent to court to answer for his misdeeds but the scandal revealed he had mental health problems. He not only took to cross-dressing but also to self-mutilation because he wanted to change gender. He was diagnosed with schizophrenia and declared unfit to stand for trial due to insanity.

The episode is commonly referred to as the 'Peter Young affair'. It had many consequences for the UK's mutual fund industry and taught financial regulators, asset management firms and fund managers important lessons. But the regulatory, institutional and moral issues raised by the scandal obscure a much more elemental feature that often escapes attention. The affair illustrates, better than perhaps any other episode, that a mutual fund's fortunes turn on its manager's attributes – his psychology, intellect, judgement, character and experience, all of which vary from one individual to the next.

In Peter Young's case, unseen psychological problems contributed to a disaster that could have cost investors dear. Thankfully, fund managers rarely have such pathological character flaws. But other, less extreme variations in psychology, intellect, judgement and experience abound. For example, some fund managers have iron strong temperaments. They see calmly through sometimes wild short-term swings in stock prices that leave weaker managers flailing. Some managers have superior analytical skills that enable them to collate information and make good judgements about whether to buy or sell a stock. Some are highly experienced and so are better able to avoid the common mistakes that plague less worldly-wise investors. Each fund manager has these attributes to different degrees, and they determine how good a job he or she can do for their investors.

Against the Tide's conceptual foundation is the dependence of a fund's performance on the skill of its active fund manager. Of course, fund managers do not work alone in darkened rooms illuminated only by flickering trading screens. On the contrary, they usually work in teams, sometimes for giant investment firms with large numbers of specialist analysts feeding them information. The better the quality of the team, the better chance the fund manager has of doing well – but only if he or she personally makes good judgements. The information they get from their team can inform those judgements, but the team does not make the final call. There are many examples of fund managers who perform very differently from their colleagues even though they work at the same company and benefit from the research of the same team. The differences in performance are explained by the simple fact that some make better judgments than others.

Unfortunately, highly skilled fund managers are few and far between. Most professional investors are swamped by the ebb and flow of the stockmarket, while only a small minority can break free of the tide. The problem is, just how do you identify skilled fund managers? After all, investment firms advertise mutual funds based on their past performance. Such adverts often tell you little or nothing about the manager of the fund. Nor can you infer anything about the current manager's skill without extra information. For example, suppose a firm runs an advert to promote a fund with a good three-year performance record. You might assume this means the current manager of the fund, call him Tom, is a skilled stock-picker. But this might not be the case. It could be that Tom took over recently because his predecessor, Tim, the man responsible for the fund's good figures, was poached by a rival firm. In that case, how do you go about deciding if Tom is a good manager whom you can trust with your money? You would need to know which funds Tom ran in the past, when he ran them and how they fared. But just how do you find that out?

Typically, only insiders – a select few mutual fund analysts – can distinguish good managers from the also-rans. They track the performance of fund managers as they move from one job to the next, taking note of how they perform at each fund. Normally this is an instinctive, back-of-the-envelope calculation or simply an insider's memory of who did what and when. This enables the insiders to build up a picture of the managers' true ability. It is very valuable and jealously guarded information. For example, if a good manager quits a fund to join a rival, an insider will sometimes decide to follow the manager by shifting his investment, too. In contrast, the majority of the fund's small investors will know nothing about the manager change or the option of switching to ensure their investments perform optimally. Knowledge, as ever, is power.

Citywire, the publisher of *Against the Tide*, has pioneered a way to lift the lid on the insiders' secrets. In 1999 it set about creating a systematic league table of fund manager, as opposed to fund, performance. The service, the Citywire Funds Insider (CFI) database, now covers 3000 fund managers across a number of countries. The database and related tools provide detailed information about fund manager performance over a variety of time periods, from one month to five years. Citywire uses the information to identify the best managers and investigate the way they work in a bid to illuminate why they are so successful.

Against the Tide continues this process by profiling some of the very best managers Citywire has come across. There are 12 chapters in the book, each profiling the background and stock-picking techniques of a different fund manager based on wide-ranging, searching interviews. None of the chapters presupposes that you have read other parts of the book, so you can read from cover to cover or focus on the chapters that interest you most. The profiles demystify the techniques of successful managers, throwing light on how the people you trust with your money ply their trade. They also reveal that a rich diversity of investment techniques can successfully beat the stockmarket – in the right hands, of course.

Against the Tide's first chapter profiles William H Miller III, one of America's finest fund managers. He is an exponent of value investing, the technique of buying bargain-priced stocks. Miller's ability to beat the stockmarket consistently at the helm of massive funds, using a very distinctive and occasionally controversial brand of value investing, is remarkable. The second chapter focuses on UK fund manager Nigel Thomas. He practises a brand of growth investing referred to by the acronym 'Garp', which stands for 'growth at a reasonable price'. Growth investors such as Thomas focus on identifying companies with the ability to earn ever larger sums of money. Such financial success should deliver a big increase in their share prices. Thomas believes that if you take the risk of investing in shares then you should aim for excellent returns to compensate for that risk, which is just what he has delivered.

Chapter three profiles Anthony Bolton, a UK fund manager who has established a breathtaking investment record over a long career. Bolton is known as a 'special situations' investor, which means he looks for stocks with certain specific characteristics. He believes those characteristics increase your chances of making big returns, and he has been proved right. The manager in the fourth chapter is Edward Bonham Carter, whose surname you may recognise since he is the brother of British actress Helena Bonham Carter. He has stolen some of his sister's spotlight, at least in this book, for his fund management prowess. Bonham Carter's style of investing is to ferret out undervalued shares, a technique with roots in value investing.

All these managers, in one form or another, are stock-pickers. They find investments by analysing companies to see if their shares present an attractive investment opportunity. Ashton Bradbury, who features in the fifth chapter, adopts a different approach. He, too, analyses companies, but he also spends a lot of time investigating the state of the economy. Bradbury aims to refine his investments to suit the economy using a technique known as 'business cycle investing'. The idea is that the economy goes through a repeating cycle of expansion followed by slower growth or recession. Different types of stock do well in different stages of the cycle, a phenomenon Bradbury tries to exploit.

Chapters six and seven present a contrast between managers specialising in different sizes of stock. First comes Kent Shepherd, who invests in US companies with large stockmarket capitalisations. Shepherd is a value investor and a contrarian, which means he tends to buy or sell a stock just when most investors are doing the opposite. Chapter seven profiles Harry Nimmo, who works at the opposite end of spectrum since he invests in firms with small market capitalisations. Nimmo deploys a distinctively rigorous approach to finding

UK smaller company stocks from his base in Scotland. Large and small stocks present investors with very different challenges and opportunities, as both chapters reveal.

David Ross, the manager profiled in chapter eight, studied the esoteric and difficult topic of quantum physics at university. He now uses the mathematical skills he developed to figure out how to invest in the stockmarket. Ross practises a technique known as 'active quantitative investing', which involves using high-powered computers and mathematical models to forecast how much money a stock could make in the future. In contrast, Anthony Nutt in chapter nine practises the much more traditional and long-established technique of income investing. Nutt invests in stocks to make money from the dividends they pay, not just from an increase in their prices. Stock dividends are very important for good long-term stockmarket returns, as the chapter makes clear.

The last three chapters further increase the diversity of investment styles in *Against the Tide*. Chapters 10 and 11 feature two investors who buy and sell a firm's bonds rather than its shares, but in two very different ways. Jonathan Platt in chapter 10 reveals how he makes money by investing in bonds issued by financially healthy companies. Platt is one of the UK's most experienced bond investors. Chapter 11 profiles David Winters, a US fund manager who seeks to make money by investing in bonds issued by bankrupt or troubled companies. Many private investors have little idea that the risky process of investing in bankrupt companies can deliver rich rewards.

Finally, chapter 12 features the team of David Huyton, Michael Lozowski and Nick Cavalla at the Man Group. This triumvirate of physicists and mathematicians differs from the rest of the managers in this book in two respects. Firstly, they deal in the world of hedge funds. These are complex products designed to make money no matter whether the stockmarket is falling or rising. Secondly, they pick and blend fund managers rather than stocks, in a bid to deliver superior returns.

The fund managers profiled in this book demonstrate that there are multifarious ways of delivering superb investment returns. The common thread is that they are all prepared to swim against the tide.

Bill Miller
In Search of Value

by Sunil Jagtiani

*V*alue investing is the highly popular art of buying stocks for much less than they are worth. It is supposed to lead to substantial capital gains once the stockmarket realises the true worth of undervalued shares. The technique is one of the oldest and most successful forms of stock-picking investors will come across. This chapter explores value investing through one its most successful exponents, US fund manager Bill Miller, and goes on to look at the history and diversity of value investing techniques.

Part 1

Miller's Winning Streak

William H Miller III, better known as plain old Bill Miller, is one of the most successful fund managers America has ever produced. He has built his reputation at Legg Mason, an investment firm with its headquarters in Baltimore, as the manager of the $12 billion Legg Mason Value Trust. Under Miller the Value Trust has beaten the US stockmarket, as measured by the performance of the S&P 500 index, for 12 consecutive years from 1991 to 2002. It is a winning streak unmatched by any other professional stock-picker since at least the 1960s. Quite possibly, no other US money manager has ever achieved a similar feat. Miller's performance looks equally impressive when you figure out the cumulative gain he has delivered for long-term investors. For example, if you had put $1000 into the Value Trust in December 1990, when Miller became its sole manager, it would have been worth $7500 in late 2003, a rise of 650%. This compares with only $4000 if your investment had risen in value by the same percentage as the S&P 500 index. The fund outstripped the average performance of its rivals by more than $3000 over the same period.

Fittingly for a man with a natural gift for investing, Miller was barely out of short trousers when he first became aware of the stock-market. 'I got interested at the age of nine or 10, in the late 1950s,' he says. 'I was out mowing the lawn and when I went in my father was looking at the stock pages. I asked, "What's that?" He said, "If you owned a piece of that company, then today you'd have made a quarter." I asked what you had to do to make that money and he said nothing, it does it by itself. Now I'd been mowing the grass for three hours to get a quarter and here you didn't have to do anything – that's the business I wanted to be in. Of course, as I learned later, you don't have to do anything to earn the rate of return delivered by the broad stockmarket, but it's a lot of work to earn above the market rate of return. That really is where the work comes in.'

Miller's childhood interest in finance eventually led him to take a degree in Economics, a subject commonly studied by fund managers. However, his path into the asset management industry after his degree was anything but conventional. Miller had already signed up for the US Army's officer training corps by the time he graduated from Washington & Lee University in 1972. Later, with the Vietnam War still raging, he was drafted into military intelligence. When the US pulled out of Vietnam in 1975 he was able to leave the army and choose a civilian career. It would be natural to think that he approached an investment firm straightaway. Instead, Miller decided he wanted to become, of all things, a Professor of Philosophy, a discipline better known for inquiring into the metaphysics of the universe rather than the construction of successful stock portfolios.

'Initially I never had much of an interest in philosophy because I got the impression that philosophy majors were kind of weaselly,' Miller says. 'But I happened to take a course in the philosophy of language as part of my undergraduate degree. That was actually quite rigorous – it wasn't about the meaning of life and that kind of thing. When I was in the army I read quite a lot of philosophy. So in 1975 I applied to Johns Hopkins University in Baltimore to undertake a Philosophy PhD. I had to submit three samples of philosophical work

---

BILL MILLER: THE MAN

Bill Miller was born in 1950 and graduated in Economics from Washington and Lee University in 1972. He is married with two children, and is a keen baseball fan.

as I didn't have an undergraduate degree in philosophy. As it turned
out, the decision to study the subject wasn't the best one to make economically. Moreover, the job market for philosophers at the time
wasn't that great. When I was in my third year of graduate school, my
adviser told me it would be tough to get a teaching job at a good university and that I could bounce from job to job. He pointed out that I
was always looking at the stockmarket and reading the financial pages
of newspapers. He asked if I'd thought about going into business. I
said, "Yes, more so now than five minutes ago."'

So in the late 1970s Miller left academia to join JE Baker, a
Pennsylvania-based firm. Eventually, he became the company's treasurer, which included responsibility for overseeing the company's
pension fund managers and running an internal portfolio. Not long
after, he was offered a job at Legg Mason by its chairman Chip Mason.
After six months of negotiation he joined the firm in 1981. Mason's
decision to recruit Miller was partly influenced by the performance of
the latter's personal stock portfolio. 'When I was in the army some
friends of mine from college sent me some money to invest for them,'
he recalls. 'Chip had asked if I'd ever invested and I told him I had this
little partnership that had done very well. So there was some empirical evidence around to help him make his decision.' A year later Miller
was appointed co-manager of the Value Trust when it was launched
in 1982, and became sole manager of the fund in 1990.

Miller's fund management style is the product of an eclectic web
of influences, possibly the most complex web of all the managers
featured in *Against the Tide*. Two elements of the web include the
techniques of other fund managers and erudite academic research. We
can look at both factors in turn. 'I've tried to identify the best people
in fund management,' Miller says, 'namely those who have done best
with the greatest level of consistency. It's very important that their
approach be intellectually rigorous and be open to replication. It
needs to be an understandable approach that can be sustained over
time. I ended up focusing on a number of value investors, legendary
names like Ben Graham, Sir John Templeton and Warren Buffett.
From that work it seemed to me that if you're going to earn an excess

return you have to buy things for less than they are worth.

'There are other ways of course. Some investors buy expensive-looking things and hope to trade them out at a higher price, say because of a change in sentiment or psychology. But I couldn't see any way of sensibly analysing and replicating such an approach. As a result I've always had a strong attachment to value investing. However, I've studied successful investors with other styles, for example George Soros, who profits from his analysis of economic trends, and Peter Lynch of Fidelity Magellan fame, a growth investor who was sensitive to stock valuations. I've looked at a number of successful investment strategies and styles, and tried to adapt them to my own approach to fund management. I think I have an approach that is very good at capturing the essence of other managers' processes.'

Many other fund managers have been influenced by men such as Graham and Buffett but, unlike Miller, few devote much of their time to reading academic research. Miller spends time digesting a range of academic papers, both financial and non-financial. For example, he sits on the board of the Santa Fe Institute, a private, not-for-profit, multi-disciplinary research organisation located in New Mexico. Some of the work produced by the Institute's academics helps Miller to view the stockmarket in new and fruitful ways. 'It's illuminating work. It helps you to think about things differently and it helps to improve

Source: Lipper

your performance,' Miller says. 'For instance, we spent a lot of time in the mid- and late-1990s analysing technology stocks, to see if they provided good value and to get a handle on how risky they might be. The work of Brian Arthur at Santa Fe on something called "path-dependence and lock-in" really helped us with our analysis. It gave us a better way to frame the consequences of rapid technological change for technology companies. Many value investors don't own technology stocks because they believe they just can't say how rapid changes in technology will affect technology companies in five or 10 years' time. Well, Arthur's work showed that, while changes in technology might be rapid, the market shares of dominant technology companies did not change that much.

'To better understand his point, take a non-technology firm such as Coke. Suppose it had to introduce a new product every two or three years and throw the old one away. Some investors would turn away from the firm because of their doubts over how those new products would do. That's one way to look at it. The other is that no matter what they introduce they're still going to have the same 47% market share. Now, come back to technology firms and take a look at anti-trust actions. They don't go and break up Coke. What do they break up? AT&T, IBM, Microsoft – all the major anti-trust actions have been against technology companies, because of market shares. Microsoft and Intel have 85-90% market shares, while Coke and Nike have much less of their markets. So, when technology stocks got cheap in the mid-1990s, Arthur's work contributed to our view that they weren't as risky as people thought.' Miller went on to make notable and highly successful investments in technology firms such as Amazon, Dell and AOL, which have been key to Value Trust's success.

CAREER PROFILE

- 1978-1981: A variety of roles at JE Baker.
- 1981-present: Fund manager at Legg Mason. Miller manages about $29 billion invested across a variety of funds, one of which, the Legg Mason Value Trust, made his name.

Some readers may wonder how technology stocks, usually thought of as the growth investor's staple fare, found their way into Miller's Value Trust. We can answer that question by looking at Miller's formal definition of value investing. He defines it as buying businesses that trade at a large discount to their intrinsic business value. A firm's intrinsic business value, in turn, is defined as the present value of the company's future free cashflow. Free cashflow basically refers to the amount of money a firm has left once you subtract all the costs of its operations. Healthy and rising levels of cashflow indicate a successful firm. Miller projects future cashflow levels and works back to see what a company's shares should be worth based on that projection. He looks for firms trading at prices materially below the levels implied by his free cashflow projections. Clearly, any stock – technology or non-technology – can trade at a large discount to its intrinsic business value and so present an investment opportunity. Put more simply, any stock can trade at a price that looks cheap compared to what the business is actually worth. So Miller is prepared to back technology firms if the investment argument is strong enough.

Of course, working out a firm's intrinsic value is not as simple as it sounds, since projecting future free cashflow levels is both an art and a science. 'When you calculate a firm's future free cashflow levels, your calculation is very sensitive to inputs,' Miller says. 'You need to build a matrix of scenarios for a firm and then determine the central tendency of your cashflow projections. We also look at a host of other valuation measures to appraise a company, such as price-to-earnings, price-to-book and price-to-cashflow ratios, to name but a few. We don't *rely* on any one of them – we look at all of them. Analysing a company's future prospects is a hard thing to do consistently well. We try to ensure our investment process is organised in such a way that

---

INVESTMENT STYLE

Miller is an eclectic contrarian who seeks to buy businesses trading at a large discount to their intrinsic value, where intrinsic value is defined as the present value of the company's future free cashflow.

it increases our chances of making good predictions. Many people don't do that – they don't say, "We have all this information, but how much of it is actually relevant to making judgements about the future?"

'Mapping past to future to find mispriced stocks is the key skill. I tell my analysts that 100% of the information we have about a company reports the past, but that 100% of any value it offers depends on the future. I think this is part of what marks us out as different from other value investors. For example, the average value investor will look 80% at historical measures and 20% at the future, whereas our split might be 50-50 or even 20-80. There's another important difference – we're constantly looking to see if we're wrong, not if we're right. A stock's in the portfolio because we believe that's right. We don't need further evidence for that. We need evidence that we're wrong, that's what we're testing for.'

Miller applies his distinctive brand of value investing to a giant sum, some $29 billion altogether. About $22 billion is accounted for by the Value Trust together with other funds with the same investment portfolio. So, in essence, we can view that $22 billion as invested in one portfolio. That portfolio typically features between 30 and 35 stocks, which means Miller makes sizeable investments in large companies. 'It's a lot of assets in a small number of stocks,' as he puts it, somewhat understating his position. We can take his largest holding from late 2003 as an example. The stock in question, online retailer Amazon, had at the time a market capitalisation of about $21 billion. Legg Mason was the biggest institutional shareholder in Amazon with well over $2 billion worth of the firm's shares. The only investor with a bigger shareholding was Amazon's founder Jeff Bezos.

The size of Miller's stock investments naturally place certain constraints on his room for manoeuvre. For instance, such large positions cannot be built up or disposed of easily or quickly. So, unsurprisingly, Miller is a long-term investor who keeps a stock in his fund for seven years on average. But, in return, he feels he gains more credibility with the senior management teams of the firms he invests in compared with less committed investors. This allows him to advise them on how he believes they can best deliver long-term shareholder value. For instance, Miller suggested to Bezos that Amazon should change the way it gave shares to its employees as part of their salary and benefits package. Miller argued for restricted stock, which is stock given to an employee over a number of years. The idea is that restricted stock should keep employees loyal and focused on delivering a rising share price over the long term. The alternative, stock options, are more complicated, harder to cost up in a firm's balance sheet and can encourage employees to focus on short-term gains. Bezos switched to restricted stock at the end of 2002. 'I think we had an influence on Amazon's decision,' Miller says. 'In fact, we have constructive dialogue with many of our management teams. But it's important to note that we're not forcing them to do something they don't want to do. All we're doing is reinforcing a certain position.'

Typically, Miller adds or removes only one or two stocks from his portfolio each year. The universe of US shares he can select from is typically contained within the S&P 500. They are very well researched by scores of analysts, so the onus is on Miller and his team to think about them creatively to find mispriced stocks. New investment ideas can arise from a number of sources, including Legg Mason's internal analysts and external brokers. Miller and his team also screen stock prices to see which firms have posted notable falls in case they have come back to levels the team would consider cheap. 'I try to give my team of analysts the names of companies I'd like them to work on,' Miller says. 'But my main contribution is not so much figuring out which names go in the fund, but rather deciding how much we should invest in the stocks we want to back. The latter set of judgements is critical to determining your long-term returns.' Miller will sell an investment for one of three reasons: if its share price rises to a level he considers fair value; if a better opportunity emerges elsewhere; or if the original argument backing the investment no longer holds.

A key aspect of Miller's investment style is that he is a contrarian who often buys unpopular companies. Some of the companies he backs have been the subject of high-profile upheaval, even scandal, and are positively disliked, not just unloved. For Miller, such 'blow-ups' can cause share prices to sink too far and have created some of his most fruitful investment opportunities. Even so, experts and non-experts alike often criticise his decision to back unpopular firms or companies perceived to be in distress. The point is very well made by a graphic published in 2002 by *Money Magazine*. The graphic was designed to look like a poster for a 1950s 'B' horror film and described the Legg Mason Value Trust as 'the scariest portfolio ever!' in quivering blood-red letters. It went on to say, 'It seems like a mild-mannered fund. But appearances can be deceiving. What surprises lurk inside?' Just to ram home the point the mocked-up poster ended with three capitalised, underlined words: 'Shocking! Amazing! Outperforming?'

However, Miller thinks critics who baulk at his contrarian streak are wrong to do so. 'Viable businesses surrounded by a fog of scandal or fear are probably mispriced,' he says baldly. 'Your default position should be that you buy them. In fact, often you will find that the more pessimistic people get, the more optimistic we become, and vice-versa. As a basic overlay, the tendency is that when news is bad, there's opportunity there, not risk, and when the news is good, there's risk and not necessarily opportunity to make a lot of money. The point is that investors overreact to dramatic news, whether it be positive or negative. That's something we try to systematically exploit.'

Moreover, if Miller is convinced that a firm is a good investment, he will continue to buy its shares even if they slide in value. The reasoning is that if the investment case is sound, the shares offer better value the lower their price falls. Once he has completed building a position in a firm, he will look at the average price he paid for his shares to judge how well he has done. Indeed, he can often be heard to say that 'lowest average cost wins'. To see how this works, we can look at the way he built up his position in Amazon between 1999, when the online retailer floated on the stockmarket, and 2001. He bought Amazon shares for a variety of prices, from more than $80 to less than $8. His decision to buy the stock as its price fell from about $40 in mid-2000 all the way down to below $8 earned him a lot of criticism. However, picking up Amazon shares at lower prices cut the average cost Miller incurred to just under $20 per share, whereas Amazon's stock price in the last quarter of 2003 reached $61, a gain of 205%.

There are numerous other examples of contrarian investments in Value Trust, such as diversified conglomerate Tyco International, the subject of a scandal in 2002, telecommunications firm Nextel, which is burdened by a large debt load, and Tenet Healthcare, also the subject of a scandal. There will be many more contrarian investments in the future, too, when new scandals break. Onlookers will continue to question Miller's decisions as emotions run high in the teeth of the as-yet-unseen blow-ups. Yet all Miller tries to do is assess a firm's prospects rationally rather than emotionally. He simply wants to buy shares trading for less than they should be. And, whatever critics might say, it is a brand of value investing that has proved singularly successful.

Part 2

The Value Approach

The first man to set out the principles of value investing systematically was Benjamin Graham, a legendary figure often described as the father of the technique. His life as an investor, teacher and writer was hugely influential. Take one of his students, none other than billionaire Warren Buffett, the chairman of Berkshire Hathaway and one of America's richest men. Buffett learned his investment techniques in Graham's classes at Columbia University. He went on to become a wildly successful value investor. Berkshire Hathaway's share price was about $12 when Buffett took it over in 1965. He used the firm to invest in stocks and to acquire businesses. In the last quarter of 2003 Berkshire Hathaway's share price was $76,000, a rise of over 630,000% since 1965. The chances of another investor ever matching his record are slim. Buffett readily acknowledges the debt he owes to Graham's teaching and advice for the level of success Berkshire Hathaway has enjoyed.

Graham was born in London in 1894 but his family moved to New York not long after. Money was tight during his childhood but he still managed to attain a scholarship to Columbia University. He graduated in 1914, turned down teaching posts at the university and took a job with a Wall Street firm. He soon established his credentials as an astute investor, but lost a fortune when the stockmarket crashed in 1929. He staved off bankruptcy and repaired his bank balance, but the crash left a lasting mark. It impressed on him the difference between speculating and investing, and the need for what he went on to call a 'margin of safety'. The latter is simply the safety offered by a stock purchased for much less than it is worth. His theories are spelled out in his seminal works, *Security Analysis* and *The Intelligent Investor*. They are as popular now as they were during Graham's lifetime, which came to an end in 1976.

Value investing in all its different forms is built on one simple but powerful injunction: buy stocks priced at less than they are worth. Like many of the core rules of investment, it is an injunction that looks obvious and banal. Yet it is equally palpable that investors ignore it, as the cycle of stockmarket boom and bust reveals. Greed leads many investors to buy stocks for much more than they are worth when optimism is high, and to sell them for much less than they are worth when pessimism reigns, resulting in painful losses. The minority of skilled investors who take the lessons of value investing seriously, men like Bill Miller, seek to use this never-ending ebb and flow in stock prices to buy low and sell high, exactly what the wider herd of overly emotional investors fails to do.

Just how do you find stocks priced at less then they are worth? Put simply, figure out how well a business is performing now, how well it is set to do in the future and whether its current share price reflects the level of success it enjoys and is likely to enjoy. Of course, this general outline has spawned many different value investing tech-niques. Some investors look for stocks paying a high current dividend yield. Others focus on a stock's likely future dividend payments to determine if its current price is attractive. Some pay more attention to finding stocks with low valuation measures, such as low price-to-earnings or price-to-book ratios. Still others, like Miller, seek to assess whether a firm's share price reflects its intrinsic value. Value investors are typically devout contrarians, too, for example Anthony Bolton, profiled in chapter three, whose hugely successful investment style is organised around five contrarian investment themes.

Many expert commentators contend that value investing is the most successful approach to the stockmarket ever devised. Some aca-demics have even tried to quantify the performance of value stocks against growth stocks. For example, three London Business School academics, Elroy Dimson, Paul Marsh and Mike Staunton, have constructed value and growth stock indices dating back to the start of the 20th Century. Their research shows that £1 invested in 1900 in their value index of companies with high dividend yields was worth more than £61,000 by the end of 2000. In contrast, the same amount invested in their growth index of lower yielding stocks was worth a little over £4000, while the stockmarket as a whole delivered a little over £16,000. Nevertheless, not everyone agrees that value stocks have substantially outperformed growth stocks. Whatever the truth of the debate, one thing is clear: value investing has proved a highly successful way to invest in the stockmarket for some expert stock-pickers, as the example of William H Miller III shows.

Nigel Thomas
Growth at a Reasonable Price

by Sunil Jagtiani

*T*he phrase 'growth at a reasonable price', usually shortened to 'Garp', sounds like such a simple investment homily that it almost seems vacuous. Surely most investors want to buy reasonably priced stock in good firms whose success will deliver capital gains for shareholders? True, but there is a lot more to successful Garp investing than the homily appears to suggest. Honest investors, after all, will admit that it is a strategy which is devilishly difficult to implement successfully. This chapter aims to illustrate these subtleties in two ways. Firstly, it examines the investment techniques of highly accomplished UK fund manager Nigel Thomas, to show what a rewarding approach Garp investing can be. Secondly, it revisits an extraordinary stockmarket period when investors paid the consequences for seeking 'Gasp', or growth at stupid prices, to show that Garp investing can provide a bulwark against dangerous excesses.

Part 1

Garp and
Nigel Thomas

G rowth at a reasonable price (Garp) investing is an extremely
popular approach to stock-picking. Type the phrase into the
Google Internet search engine and it will churn out 4500
results from web pages run by firms and investors all over the world.
It also has a relatively long stockmarket tradition. The term 'Garp'
was first coined in the early 1970s by Eddie C Brown, an African-
American born to a 13-year-old mother in a Florida trailer park, who
beat the odds to become a leading US fund manager. But though he
coined the acronym, he is not Garp investing's best-known practi-
tioner. That accolade belongs to investment legend Peter Lynch. He
ran the Fidelity Magellan fund from the late 1970s, taking it from a
size of $20 million to about $14 billion, with a million shareholders,
by the time he retired in 1990, aged 46. Lynch delivered an outstanding return of about 2500%, nearly six times better than the US
stockmarket's return over the same period. Little wonder he boosted
the popularity of Garp investing.

In contrast to Lynch's growing fame, few took notice when a little-
known fund manager, Nigel Thomas, launched a fund called Pembroke
UK Growth in the mid-1980s. He was working for the small London-
based stockbroker John Carrington & Co, which was co-founded by
John Carrington, a journalist turned fund manager who used to write
a stock-picking column for *The Times*. By 2002 Thomas had established himself as one of the best-ever fund managers, and his name

was splashed across the national press as two leading UK investment houses battled in court to retain his services. If ever someone denies that the skills of an individual fund manager are key to investment success, the story of Nigel Thomas' career serves as the ideal riposte.

Thomas, who was born in March 1955, joined fund managers John Carrington & Co as a portfolio manager in 1979. Thomas describes Carrington, who retired in 1996 at the age of 55, as a mentor and a major influence on his fund management skills. 'John Carrington taught me a lot of what I know today,' Thomas says. 'Everyone needs a good teacher, and he was mine.'

Thomas launched Pembroke UK Growth in 1986 and ran it in one guise or another for 15 years. The fund went through two name changes, the first when Dutch firm ABN Amro Asset Management bought Carrington's business in 1997 and renamed the fund ABN Amro UK Growth, and the second when UK investment house Artemis Fund Managers merged with ABN Amro Asset Management in 2002 and renamed the fund Artemis Capital. But whatever the fund happens to be called, and whoever runs it in the future, it will be remembered for many years to come for its outstanding success under Thomas.

Between 1986 and mid-2002, when Thomas relinquished control, Artemis Capital posted a massive rise of – wait for it – 1020%. To put it another way, an investor prescient enough to place £1000 in the fund at its launch would have had £11,200 by mid-2002. A similar amount invested in a fund that passively tracks the movements of the UK stockmarket would have risen to about £5000, while £1000 left in a deposit account would have become just £3500. Thomas also ran a portfolio that became the country's best performing UK equity fund during the stockmarket boom of late 1999 and early 2000. The fund, Solus UK Special Situations, rose 324% under his guidance from 1996 to late 2000. The UK stockmarket rose by 82% over the same period,

NIGEL THOMAS: THE MAN

Nigel Thomas was born in 1955 and is married with two children. A keen horse-racing and football fan, he is a supporter of Ipswich Town.

while UK equity funds on average posted a marginally better return of 83%. So, while Thomas may have the odd bad period, his long-term personal fund management career record is simply outstanding.

Thomas now plies his trade at Framlington, a London-based investment house established in 1969, which manages about £2.9 billion worth of assets for private investors and institutions. He joined the firm in September 2002 and took on the Framlington UK Select Opportunities fund. Put so baldly, the transition from his previous employer, ABN Amro Asset Management, to Framlington sounds like a straightforward process. But that was far from the case. Thomas worked for ABN Amro from 1997, the year the Dutch firm acquired Carrington's business. By April 2002 ABN Amro's UK fund range had developed a reputation for excellence under Thomas and his long-time colleague George Luckraft, a gifted fund manager himself. The two men were responsible for more than £1 billion worth of assets, and were integral to the company's success. Yet in the same month they shocked the UK's investment funds industry by tendering their resignations. By the end of May 2002 both men had walked out to join Framlington. However, ABN Amro claimed that they were in breach of contracts stipulating a 12-month notice period.

The dispute swiftly ended up in court. ABN Amro took out court injunctions to stop Thomas and Luckraft working at Framlington. Just 24 hours later both men agreed to comply with the request as part of a deal to lift the injunctions, pending a High Court trial. Thankfully Thomas, Luckraft and ABN Amro managed to resolve their differences a week before the trial was due to start. Just why the dispute flared up will remain unknown, locked behind confidentiality agreements signed by all parties. But rarely had a tussle over the services of fund managers led to such a contretemps. It is a saga that shows just how important talented fund managers become to their employers. Investment excellence is very hard to secure, and though the team around a good stock-picker provides a great deal of useful assistance, in the final analysis the skill of the fund manager is key.

Thomas cites Lynch, the leading exponent of Garp investing mentioned earlier, as a major influence on his fund management style. The ex-Fidelity manager's books on growth investing form part of Thomas' financial library at his home in East Bergholt, Suffolk, where he retreats to write the regular reports due to his fund's shareholders. 'I respect Peter Lynch,' Thomas says, 'and I do very similar things. Lynch once said you can't forecast a stockmarket index. He said if you spend 12 minutes a year predicting where the stockmarket is going you've wasted 10 of those minutes.' Like most serious investors, he reads the words of Warren Buffett, too. A little more unusual is his penchant for quoting economist John Maynard Keynes. Thomas' interest lies in Keynes' investment, rather than economic, insight, since Keynes built up a good performance record both for King's College, Cambridge, and the private firms that retained his services.

Underlying Thomas' approach to fund management is the belief that investors who opt to take the risks associated with investing in equities deserve commensurate rewards. He will range across the stockmarket, looking at stocks of any size, for investments he finds attractive. He calls it a 'multi-cap' approach and says he learned it from his time working at John Carrington & Co. Sometimes he finds

GROWTH AT A REASONABLE PRICE

Garp investing, like growth investing, aims for substantial capital gains from shares in companies with above average earnings per share compared with the wider stockmarket. But Garp investors also have an eye on value. They look for growth stocks but do not want to pay too much for them, and use earnings per share growth to help make that judgement. They stipulate that a stock's percentage rate of annual earnings growth should exceed its price per earnings, or P/E, ratio. Some use a variant of the P/E ratio, the PEG ratio, to express this idea formally. The PEG ratio divides a stock's P/E by its percentage earnings growth figure. A stock whose percentage earnings growth level exceeds its P/E will have a PEG ratio of less than 1, the cut-off point for many Garp proponents. More generally, Garp investing lies around the mid-point of the continuum between pure growth and pure value investing. It can cover any type of stock, not just technology firms as some investors assume, and it can range over firms of any size, though most growth investors tend to favour companies with smaller or mid-sized market capitalisations.

more value in small and mid-sized stocks; in other periods large blue chips in the FTSE 100 index catch his eye. Thomas is prepared to rotate his portfolio appropriately, and such flexibility and pragmatism are defining characteristics of his investment style.

Thomas is very much a stock-picker, spending his time poring over individual companies to assess their worth as investments. Like most successful fund managers he studies the economy and notes its trends, but it does not form the basis of his investment decisions. He has a company-centred, bottom-up style rather than an economy-focused, top-down approach.

Thomas does not use strict PEG ratios to select investments, but describes his valuation methods as very similar. 'I tend to like companies where the P/E is below the earnings growth rate,' he says. 'Ideally you want the best of both worlds, a healthy and sustainable earnings growth rate and P/E expansion at the same time. What you do is take a view on the growth rate over the next two or three years and extrapolate back to ask what the P/E should be. Then you ask if the firm is mispriced. You're using objective and subjective views about forward earnings growth to say the P/E is x, the earnings growth rate is y, so is this mispriced?' For Thomas, a stock's earnings per share growth is crucial to the overall capital return he can deliver for investors, since earnings fund dividend payments that can be reinvested into more stock. 'Without earnings per share growth you don't get dividend growth,' he points out, 'and over the last century the bulk of the return on equities, nearly three-quarters, has come from reinvested dividends.'

However, if you force Thomas to identify what he views as the

---

CAREER PROFILE

- 1979-1984: Fund manager at John Carrington & Co.
- 1984-1986: Fund manager at Hill Samuel Asset Management.
- 1986-2002: Fund manager ABN Amro Asset Management, where he made his name managing the ABN Amro UK Growth fund.
- 2002-present: Fund manager at Framlington, where he runs, and has his pension invested in, the Framlington UK Select Opportunities fund.

secret of his success, he will most likely refer to his parsimony about stock losses. 'The secret to making money in the stockmarket is to lose the least when you get it wrong,' he says. 'I often look at the risks of an investment rather than just the money I think I might stand to make from it. The latter will take care of itself if you back the right firms. But always cut your losses and use that capital elsewhere. You have to be able to admit that you've made a mistake, since bad companies will compound losses. If you've made a mistake for any reason, whether it's misjudging management teams or a firm's strategy, or if a company isn't returning analysts' phone calls – that can be a great alert signal! – cut your losses. Take the money out and invest it where you think it will get a better return. Don't worry if you're selling each pound you invested in the stock for 50p, since that stock could be 50p in five years' time, which means the opportunity cost of tying your capital up in that stock is high. Instead, deploy that 50p in a company that goes to 150p over five years.'

Claims Direct, once the highest-profile personal injury claims specialist in the UK, provides a spectacular example of Thomas' 'cut your losses' principle at work. The company was founded in December 1995 by solicitor Colin Poole and entrepreneur Tony Sullman to take on personal injury legal claims on a 'no win, no fee' basis. Regulatory changes boosted the firm's fortunes and it listed on the stockmarket in June 2000 at 180p per share after a period of substantial growth. Many commentators expected the personal injury market to mushroom, as it had done in the US, which suggested a bright future lay ahead for the firm. Thomas bought stock in the company at flotation and later at about 200p. Its share price rocketed to a peak of 360p in September 2000, valuing the firm at about £725

INVESTMENT STYLE

Thomas believes that investors who opt to take the risks associated with investing in equities deserve commensurate rewards, but he warns that they should cut their losses to ensure they lose the least when they get it wrong.

million. Claims Direct's brand was widely recognised by a British public happy to embrace the 'compensation culture' prevalent in the US. The company seemed set to become the leading player in a growing industry.

Claims Direct's business model was based on making claimants buy an insurance policy, which would pay costs, including legal fees, if their claim failed. Claimants often took out a loan from the firm to buy the policy, which cost about £1250. If the claim succeeded, Claims Direct expected the defendant's insurer to pick up the cost of the premium. The problem was that defendants' insurers began to argue the premiums were unreasonably expensive and refused to pay out. Claims Direct had to take the cost of the premium out of the damages secured by successful litigants. But this frequently left successful claimants with paltry sums, a few pounds in some cases, sparking a raft of negative press stories. One tabloid newspaper even labelled the firm 'Shames Direct', a disastrous development for an organisation that promoted itself as the people's champion. Unsurprisingly, Claims Direct's case load slumped. The company faced other financial difficulties, too, and by November 2000, only five months after flotation, the writing was on the wall when its share price collapsed from 231p to 87.5p in the space of five days.

The company eventually went bust in July 2002, when its shares

THOMAS' PERFORMANCE OVER 5 YEARS (31/08/98 - 31/08/03)

III Nigel Thomas's personal performance in the UK All Companies sector
Average fund manager performance in the UK All Companies sector
FTSE All Share Cumulative

Total Returns [%]

Month End

* For further information see p192

Source: Citywire

were suspended at 3p. Many investors were left with massive losses. In a deliciously ironic twist, some formed a class action group to sue the firm for compensation, claiming its flotation prospectus was misleading. Thomas managed to avoid such a disastrous outcome by selling his stake when he realised he had made a mistake. 'Claims Direct looked like a good business model when it floated, although the management team wasn't top drawer,' he says. 'But when the insurers stopped paying, well that blew their business model apart. I took the view that the business model wasn't robust and that the insurance industry was rebelling against it. I could see there were going to be huge cashflow problems, so I decided to cut a loss – the last time I traded in the stock I sold it at about 80p.'

Thomas' record, however, tells you he can draw on many more investment successes than failures. His company analysis process is multi-stage and involves meeting management teams, delving into reports and accounts, using analysts' research and assessing stock graphs to help time investment decisions. Countless meetings with chief executives and finance directors from sectors across the stockmarket have turned him into something of an expert on body language. 'That's actually very important,' he says. 'You sometimes find a finance director or chief executive will start to rub his eyes nervously or pull at his collar when you ask about trading conditions. It can be a sign that they are being economical with the truth.'

More generally, experience has given him the tools to size up the quality and attitude of management teams. Irish firm Baltimore Technologies, a provider of Internet security products, and one-time darling of the stockmarket boom, provides an example of just how such meetings affect his investment decisions. The firm, floated in 1999, saw it shares rocket an astonishing 1600% to £148 by March 2000, which pushed its market capitalisation past £5 billion and propelled it into the FTSE 100 index of blue-chip shares. Yet its revenues in 1999 were just £23 million and it posted a loss of £31 million for the same year. 'I bought Baltimore Technologies at £8 during the stockmarket bubble,' Thomas says. 'The Internet was growing very quickly, you needed security products, lots of us got caught up in the story. Today I can look back and recall that ABN Amro was their largest customer, yet they did just £1.5 million turnover with them. Anyway, I met Baltimore Technologies' management and I just wasn't convinced they were very good. I remember I went to a technology conference right at the peak of the market and they'd flown over in a private jet! I sold most of my shares – I began selling at £60 and my last bargain was for £100 per share.' The decision to sell was an astute call, given that Baltimore Technologies' share price fell to a low of 10p in March 2003.

However, stocks such as Baltimore Technologies are hardly typical of the investments Thomas usually makes. They belong to a very peculiar period for the stockmarket, the like of which we will not see again for decades. Instead, Thomas cites UK specialist retailer Merchant Retail, a much lower-profile firm, as a stock that typifies his investment style. The £155 million company is best known for its main subsidiary, The Perfume Shop, which sells perfume at competitive prices through 48 outlets around the UK. The firm has delivered earnings per share growth at a rate higher than its P/E ratio for a number of years, fulfilling the key requirement of a Garp investor. Between 1999 and 2002 Merchant Retail's average annual earnings per share growth was 32%, compared with a P/E ratio that averaged about 20. 'I started buying Merchant Retail in the mid-1990s at 16p,' Thomas says. 'By March 2003 they were about 145p, a rise of over 900%. They have slightly better ranges, slightly better price points and compete against a very flabby competitor, Boots, which is a general retailer of health and beauty products. Overall, specialist retailers have been a very good area for me.'

Many other successes like Merchant Retail embellish Thomas' fund management career. Some readers may review the features of his investment style and think, 'I could do that'. Thomas himself is happy to provide Buffett-like homilies to help them along. There are many, including gems such as 'buy good companies', 'admit when you've made a mistake and cut a loss', 'use your eyes and ears', 'use charts on stocks not indices' and 'remain flexible, parsimonious and pragmatic'. Yet, however much you instruct somebody in an activity, there is no guarantee he can do it at all, let alone do it well. This is partly down to experience, and Thomas can call on nearly 25 years' worth of that. But there is also something in his stock-picking ability that you simply cannot analyse away. It is variously called intuition, a gut feeling or a sixth sense for the right call at the right time. It is like a thin layer of magic dust that collects on good fund managers and is very hard to wash off. We can only hope a few specks of the stuff have found their way onto the pages of this book.

Part 2

Gasping for Growth

O n 6 March 2000 about 1800 people converged on Boston College in the US for a conference featuring some of the global economy's most powerful figures. The topic of discussion was the New Economy, a diverse group of youthful technology and Internet firms that promised to revolutionise people's lives, and whose share prices had soared. Two of the speakers were Alan Greenspan, chairman of the US Federal Reserve Board, and Arthur Levitt, head of the US Securities and Exchange Commission. Both would deliver a final warning that an explosion of speculative growth investing in New Economy stocks had driven share prices to extraordinary and questionable levels. But it was too late to avert what had become inevitable – there was but one week to go before the start of the worst bear market in modern stockmarket history.

Few investors at the time would have believed it. Many continued to revel in what seemed a golden era for growth investing, led by technology and Internet firms. After all, the global economy was booming, towed along by a US economic growth rate of 7%. Firms had just spent a breathtaking $280 billion worldwide on technology products to fix the millennium bug, to ensure their computers functioned properly when the year became 2000. Internet usage had ballooned and its far-reaching consequences for business had sent the fortunes of web firms soaring, culminating in Internet Service Provider AOL's $100 billion acquisition of media company Time Warner. The deal was the largest in corporate history, creating a firm worth more than $300 billion. The popularity of mobile telephone technology had exploded, too, with Vodafone's £100 billion hostile takeover of German mobile operator Mannesmann still fresh in the mind.

Investors were dizzied by the sums involved. They ruthlessly sold traditional, profitable firms – so-called Old Economy stocks – to fund purchases of younger technology and Internet companies. Some of the latter had little or no revenues, let alone profits, such as start-ups from Pets.com to Furniture.com, but they still posted massive share price gains. Analysts beguiled investors to commit even more cash to the stockmarket with predictions of greater riches to come. In the US the Nasdaq index, laden with technology and Internet firms, had soared 65% in the four months up to Boston College's 6 March New Economy conference. That gave the index's 5000 constituent companies a staggering market value of $6 trillion, or two-thirds the worth of the entire output of the US economy in 2000. Technology indices in the rest of the world soared, too. The UK launched the FTSE techMARK100 index with an opening value of 2000 in October 1999. It hit a high of 5743 points on the day of the Boston College conference, a rise of 187% in five months. Investors, especially growth investors, had never had it so good.

Greenspan, coincidentally celebrating his 74th birthday, probably knew from long experience that it was too good to be true. In his conference speech he said investors were 'groping for the appropriate valuations' of Internet and technology firms. 'The exceptional stock price volatility of these newer firms,' he said, 'and, in the view of some, their outsized valuations, indicate the difficulty of divining the particular technologies and business models that will prevail in the decades ahead.' US Securities and Exchange Commission chairman Levitt was much more straightforward. 'Valuing a company has never been an exact science,' he said. 'But in today's market, does it even make sense anymore to look at a P/E ratio? Are some of today's companies really worth 1000 times nothing? To justify today's valuations, some emphasise future potential and intangible assets... but any way you look at it, many of today's valuations seem to defy traditional explanation.'

Stockmarkets wobbled as these comments were reported by the press, but doubts were put to one side as the week progressed. The Nasdaq rose again and on Friday 10 March, four days after Greenspan's and Levitt's warnings, it broke through the 5000 mark to close at 5048 points. It was an historic moment, for the Nasdaq had reached its summit following two decades of unparalleled success for growth investors. But when stockbrokers and fund managers fired up their PCs the following Monday, their trading screens turned blood red, the colour of falling prices. The world's stockmarkets had tipped into what was to become one of the worst bear markets ever.

The Nasdaq lost just over half its value – a fall of more than 2500 points – by the end of 2000. It kept on falling, reaching about 1100 points in October 2002. From peak to trough the tumble was nearly 80%. The UK's juvenile FTSE techMARK 100 index fared even worse and its pain lasted longer. It fell 90% from its peak on Greenspan's 74th birthday to its low at just over 550 points in 2003. Trillions were lost around the globe and economies were pushed into recession, followed by slow, torpid recoveries as firms and investors struggled to come to terms with substantial stockmarket losses. Companies caught up in the boom's mega-mergers, such as AOL and Vodafone, posted massive, billion-dollar losses. Internet and technology companies went to the wall, leaving shareholders with nothing but regrets. The survivors, even big companies such as Yahoo!, Amazon and Cisco Systems, were worth a fraction of their peak value. Investors, especially growth investors, had rarely had it so bad.

Why did the boom and bust happen? This question will occupy commentators, stockmarket historians and academics for years to come. In one sense, investors were right to think that the Internet and other new technologies would revolutionise the way we live, work and shop. But they placed an hysterical value on the companies at the forefront of the change. In fact, growth investing had lost sight of its roots and become little more than gambling in the run-up to March 2000. Investors simply bought stock in already expensive technology and Internet firms, hoping their market capitalisations would keep on rocketing. It was as if the 'Greater Fool' theory was in operation, according to which 'foolish' investors buy expensive securities during stockmarket bubbles because they think there will be 'greater fools than me' prepared to buy them at higher prices. Meanwhile, company revenues, earnings and profits, if they were analysed robustly at all, were in effect paid only lip service. Seduced by the lure of apparently easy and substantial capital gains, investors chased growth at ridiculous prices.

But growth investing is supposed to be built on a reasoned assessment of a firm's earnings prospects. It is traditionally defined as a style of investing that aims for substantial capital gains by seeking out firms with higher than average earnings per share compared with the wider stockmarket. The theory is that higher average earnings swell a stock's market capitalisation over time. Moreover, Garp investing warns investors not to pay over the odds for a growth story. If only investors had sought growth at a reasonable price, rather than growth at stupid prices, one of the most damaging periods in the history of the stockmarket, and the economic ills it caused, could have been avoided. In the afterglow of the white hot stockmarket bubble, chastened investors have rarely felt so keenly the desire to buy growth at reasonable rather than outlandish prices.

Anthony Bolton
Special Situations

by Sunil Jagtiani

A special situations investor is a little bit like the stockmarket's version of a thrill-seeker. This is because he or she likes to take more risk than average in the hope of a suitably valuable reward. The reward in question is a superior level of capital growth compared with less ambitious investment strategies. The term 'special situations' refers very loosely to any stock thought likely to rise in value for a particular reason, such as a new business strategy or an impending merger or takeover. The best way to gain a better understanding of the techniques involved is to analyse the fund management style of a special situations investor. There is none better than Anthony Bolton, one of the most successful fund managers ever.

Something Special

O ver the last two decades Anthony Bolton's performance as a fund manager has been, quite simply, outstanding. He is arguably the best UK-based fund manager of his generation, if not the best the country has ever produced. Some of the fund managers in this book cite him among the investors they most admire. Bolton is also one of the most powerful figures in the City of London, by dint of his massive funds and role as managing director of Fidelity Investments' UK operations. Fidelity, one of the country's largest investment firms, is able to take major shareholdings in leading firms. Bolton is prepared to use the power such a shareholding confers to make sure a company acts in what he takes to be the best interests of its investors. This was apparent in 2003 when he led a shareholders' revolt against the first proposed chairman of ITV plc, the firm created by the £4.6 billion merger of UK television companies Granada and Carlton Communications. Such power has led some to call him 'The Kingmaker' or even 'The Silent Assassin', the latter sobriquet reflecting the fact that he prefers to work behind the scenes rather than in the spotlight.

The story of Bolton's career begins in 1971, when he graduated from Trinity College, Cambridge University, with a degree in Engineering. He joined a small merchant bank, Keyser Ullmann, the same year as an investment analyst. Five years later he took his first job as a fund manager at Schlesinger Investment Management, where he successfully ran a fund investing in UK smaller companies. Bolton's big break came in 1979 when he joined Fidelity Investments just after the US firm set up in the UK. At the time the UK division had only one other fund manager. Fidelity Investments' position today as one of the UK's largest investment firms is due in no small measure to the performance of Bolton's funds.

Bolton launched Fidelity Special Situations, the fund that established his credentials as a top stock-picker, in December 1979. He has managed it ever since and few, if any, rival UK-based fund managers can claim to have managed the same fund for such a long period of time. A £1000 investment put into the fund at launch was worth nearly £81,000 by late 2003, equivalent to a staggering rise of almost 8000%. The rise in the investment would have been volatile rather than constant, because of the way Bolton manages the fund, but long-term investors have been very well rewarded for putting up with the volatility. Bolton's fund is the best performing of the 43 or so UK equity portfolios with track records stretching back to December 1979. They managed a much more modest average rise of about 2500%, while the rise in the UK stockmarket amounted to just over 1800%.

Over the years Fidelity Special Situations has attracted investors in their droves and become one of Fidelity Investment's flagship funds. By late 2003 it had assets of £2.5 billion invested in a portfolio of 190 stocks. The size of the fund is worth noting, since it is very hard to deliver good performance at the helm of a portfolio that grows from a minnow into a giant. At one stage in his Fidelity career Bolton successfully managed more than £6 billion invested in European stocks, too. This marks him out as unusual among his peers, since few modern-day fund managers concurrently run portfolios invested in

---

ANTHONY BOLTON: THE MAN

Anthony Bolton was born in 1950 and graduated with a degree in Engineering from Trinity College, Cambridge. Married with three children, one of his main interests is classical music. A keen piano player, Bolton composes music and has written pieces for his son's choir.

different geographical regions. In January 2003 Bolton decided to focus solely on Fidelity Special Situations, which he plans to manage until at least 2005.

One of the men Bolton cites as a major influence on his approach to fund management is Peter Lynch, a former Fidelity employee in the US. Lynch is well known both as a highly successful fund manager and as the author of popular investment books. Just like Bolton, Lynch turned a small fund into a giant and delivered outstanding performance along the way. Bolton and Lynch share other similarities, too. For instance, both like to invest in special situations stocks and both focus on small or medium-sized companies rather than large firms.

'Anyone who works at Fidelity can't help but be influenced by Peter Lynch,' Bolton says. 'We've met a number of times and I've read his books, which contain tons of useful information, particularly for stock-pickers. For example, one piece of advice I remember is that the more stones you turn over, the more chance you have of finding something. So we search for investment opportunities diligently and I look to have as many ideas as possible coming my way. Of course, not everything Peter says is original to him. In this business there is very little that is original – we're all borrowing information from different places and putting our own emphasis on it. But he has a facility for putting things very clearly. For instance, he says you should be able to describe why you own a stock to an intelligent 15-year-old in a few sentences. If you can't do that then it's probably not a good holding.'

Bolton says the second major influence on his approach to fund management is legendary value investor Warren Buffett, chairman of Berkshire Hathaway, who has earned himself the sobriquet 'the sage of Omaha'. 'Warren Buffett is just exceptional,' Bolton explains. 'His advice and characterisation of the stockmarket sticks in the mind. For example, one judicious piece of advice is that when you're buying a stock, consider that you're buying a whole business. His characterisation of the stockmarket as the manic depressive Mr Market is also worth recounting. It was a description penned by his teacher, Ben Graham. It encourages you to think of the stockmarket as an individual with emotional problems who sometimes offers you a stock for a ridiculously high price and at other times for a ridiculously low price. And Mr Market doesn't mind being ignored – you don't have to take the price he offers, and he'll come back with a new quote the next day. Well, the more manic depressive his behaviour, the more chance you have to make money, as long as you remember he's there to serve rather than guide you.'

Bolton is a value investor who aims for capital growth and who searches for under-priced stocks. About 80% of his fund is invested in small and medium-sized firms, with the rest in large companies. Bolton focuses on analysing individual companies, rather than 'big picture' economic or industry trends, to find attractive investments. His investment style is such that his fund advances in spurts interspersed with periods of less exciting performance. Partly this is because he is a contrarian buying unloved shares whose performance he believes is set to improve. One or two years later, if his decision to buy is proved right – and more often than not it is – he will sell those contrarian stocks when they are more popular and trading at higher prices. Bolton feels adopting a contrarian approach to stock-picking is crucial for long-term success, even if in the short term those contrarian picks fail to perform well. 'Fairly early on I understood that to be a successful investor you had to do something different, that going against the trend was the way to do better than the average investor,' he says. 'But you need to have a certain sort of mind-set that not everyone has to be a value or contrarian investor. Other things being equal, most people like to be in the herd, they like to be comfortable as part of the "in" crowd.'

What this shows, according to Bolton, is that a person's temperament is a major determinant of how successful an investor they are likely to be. 'There's a very fine line involved,' he explains. 'You need conviction and the courage to go against the crowd, but your views shouldn't be too strong. You should be prepared to change your mind. If you have very strong views that never change, well that's bad. At the other end of the spectrum if you don't have views or you oscillate in your views too easily, then that's bad. You need to be something in the middle, you need to have conviction but be prepared to change your view in the light of evidence. I've learned that from experience. Some of the greatest investors can switch views quickly, almost on a pin. They can be persuaded they are wrong.'

So we now have a general view of Bolton's approach to fund management: he is a phenomenally successful value investor with a contrarian streak, who is able to manage giant funds invested largely in small and medium-sized companies. But just how does this approach work in practice? The first feature to note is that Bolton looks for investments that fall into one of five categories: recovery plays; firms on a discount to their underlying worth; companies offering unrecognised growth potential; opportunities linked to impending corporate activity; and firms that are simply cheap compared with others in their industry. These categories represent the types of 'special situations' he looks for, and we can look at each one in detail.

Recovery plays, as their name suggests, are investments in stocks whose fortunes are at a low ebb but are set to turn around. 'Recovery turnarounds have really been one of the main themes in my UK fund,' Bolton says. 'These are firms that have done badly. Investors grow tired and fed up with them, and their share price falls. But then things start to change for the better. Very often it involves a company restructuring or a management change. Now I have to buy these stocks early. I want to be buying when people are still selling. If they work out, then buyers reappear when you want to sell. A key period for a recovery turnaround stock I'm interested in is three months before a set of poor results, which is expected to be the low in the company's fortunes. I have to buy these stocks in advance of the bad news, so that's when I'm building up a position. The stock price may still be falling when I'm buying, but in a way that's good given the size of my fund, since it means I can pick up larger quantities of shares. I have no problem buying a stock if its price is falling as long as we are on top of the situation. Once recovery turnarounds start moving up, the volume of available shares just dries up.'

Bolton cites large Anglo-Dutch publisher Reed Elsevier as an example of a recovery turnaround that has featured in his fund. He decided to invest in the firm after it hired Crispin Davies, a businessman he respected, as its chief executive in July 1999. At the time investors in the City of London were wary of the stock because Reed had posted disappointing growth and issued profit warnings. 'We'd followed Crispin closely at a previous company, Aegis, another turnaround we'd invested in,' Bolton says. 'He had a new strategy for Reed and wanted to implement a number of changes, so we decided to invest.' In the short term the company's share price struggled despite Davies' appointment. Investors were reluctant to accept that the firm's woes were set to end. Reed's shares rallied substantially during the extraordinary stockmarket boom of late 1999, but soon went into reverse when boom turned to bust. Three months into the year 2000 they languished at about 350p, not far from the lowest point they hit after Davies became chief executive. However, Davies' strategy improved the firm's fortunes, and its shares rose strongly to a high of nearly 720p in 2001. They slipped back in 2002 and 2003, but nowhere near the depressed levels of 1999. 'Reed is typical of a recovery turnaround,' Bolton says. 'Its management and strategy change eventually delivered a better share price.'

The second special situations category comprises firms trading at a discount to their underlying worth. The skill here is to audit and

---

INVESTMENT STYLE

Bolton is a contrarian value investor who organises his investments around five key themes: recovery plays; firms on a discount to their underlying worth; companies offering unrecognised growth potential; opportunities linked to impending corporate activity; and firms that are simply cheap compared to others in their industry.

value a company's assets as accurately as possible. You divide the figure you get by the number of shares in the firm, giving you each share's net asset value or underlying worth. If the firm's share price is significantly below its net asset value, it may present an investment opportunity. 'Investments in this category tend to be holding companies or property companies,' Bolton says. 'When I ran European funds I came across a number of holding companies. For example, there's a family holding company in France, FFP, which is the main shareholder in car-maker Peugeot Citroën. Most of the time FFP sells at a 45% discount to its net asset value. So if we happen to like Peugeot as an investment, why not buy the shares via the holding company at a 45% discount? What I'm looking for is something cheaply valued where people could value it differently, where the risk/return relationship is skewed in my favour – they are cheaply valued enough so that you're protected from the risk of losing too much money, but in certain circumstances you might do well.'

Firms offering unrecognised growth potential make up Bolton's third special situations category. His aim is to find a high-quality business whose share price is lower than should be the case. 'I'm looking for a good business that for some reason isn't valued highly by the stockmarket,' Bolton says. 'I often give London Stock Exchange as an example. In 2000 it became the first European stockmarket to, itself, float on the stockmarket. I looked at Australia and Singapore, whose stock exchanges were already listed, and saw that they got quite high valuations. And if you think about the London exchange, well it's basically a quasi-monopoly business. I thought it deserved to get a high valuation, and I don't think it has achieved that yet.'

Another way Bolton finds unrecognised growth is to search for a company with a fast-growing 'hidden' division. He gives Provident Financial, which specialises in door-to-door lending to people with low credit ratings, as an example. 'It was a mature business in the UK, growing at about 3%. But the firm had set up new businesses in Eastern Europe, in countries such as Hungary, the Czech Republic and Poland. Its business model seemed to work as well there as it does in the UK, and the division was profitable. I felt people were missing this growth angle and went out to Poland to see it first-hand. It confirmed my view that there was a really exciting business hidden within Provident Financial.'

Firms set for corporate activity provide the next special situations category. 'It's getting something for nothing,' Bolton says. 'I'm basically trying to find a business that has a higher chance of corporate activity, for example by looking for an opportunity in a consolidating industry. The UK market is very helpful in this regard – most UK firms are open to corporate activity, unlike many in Europe. I analyse a company's shareholders closely when I look for a corporate angle. For instance, I prefer smaller firms' shares to be concentrated in the hands of four or five institutional shareholders, which makes it easier for someone to come along and take over the firm.'

A concrete example of a firm that benefited from a corporate angle is provided by UK supermarket group Safeway, which was struggling to compete with its rivals when Bolton invested in it. He took the view that a bidder would try to buy Safeway if its management team failed to improve its fortunes. In January 2003 a bid duly came through from UK supermarket chain WM Morrison, triggering a bidding war with a number of suitors involved. Safeway's share price rose from about 210p at the time of the bid to 320p by the end of January, a gain of over 50% in just a few days.

BOLTON'S PERFORMANCE OVER 5 YEARS (31/08/98 - 31/08/03)

||| Antony Bolton Cumulative
■ FTSE All Share Cumulative   Average Manager Cumulative

* For further information see p192

Source: Citywire

Bolton's last special situations category consists of firms whose shares simply look cheap compared with rivals in their industry. 'I look at the stocks in an industry and sieve out the cheapest 10-20%,' Bolton says. 'I then ask whether they deserve to be so cheap. They may not be the best firms – often the companies I invest in aren't necessarily the best or fastest-growing – but equally they may not deserve to be so lowly valued.' The banking sector provides one example of this approach in action. Bolton took the view that Irish banking stocks, for some time the cheapest in the banking sector, were too lowly valued. 'There is an argument that the peripheral countries in Europe, like Ireland, will enjoy faster economic growth than core countries, such as Germany,' he explains. 'I buy that argument. Ireland is also the only English-speaking country in the 12-member eurozone, which I think is a very attractive factor in the long run. The country has a low tax rate, too. So it all seemed pretty unusual – you had among the most lowly valued stocks, yet they were in a country with better than average growth, lower than average tax rates and other positive factors. So I decided to invest in the Irish banking sector.'

Of course, selecting stocks in each of these categories requires a lot of detailed analysis. Bolton goes through a fixed analytic process to decide which ones he wants to buy. The process consists of the following key steps: analysing a stock's valuation, to decide if it is cheap or dear; examining a firm's balance sheet, to determine its financial health; analysing management teams, to judge their quality, to get more information about the businesses they run and to see if a company's directors are buying or selling its shares; and technical analysis, the discipline of analysing charts of a firm's share price to see what they tell you about likely future price movements.

It is physically impossible for Bolton to do all the research himself. Fidelity's large team of analysts, together with external experts, feed Bolton with much of the information he seeks. For example, Fidelity's analysts will look out for investments that fit into one of Bolton's categories, examine a stock's valuation or run through a firm's balance sheet and send the research to him. 'In the early days, when I managed smaller amounts of money and portfolios with fewer holdings, I could do much of that as an individual,' he says. 'Today I manage a very large amount of money, my fund has almost 200 holdings, and I just couldn't do all the analysis on my own. The team around me enables me to run a fund with many more holdings than would otherwise be possible – it really is a key input.' However, once he receives the information his job is to sift through it to decide if a stock is worth buying. Ultimately the performance of his fund depends on the skill with which he makes such judgements.

As most investors know, a host of valuation measures can be applied to a stock in a bid to determine if it represents a good investment. Bolton recommends investors make use of this diversity. 'What I tend to argue is that you shouldn't use or be focused on just one valuation measure,' he says. 'Different types of firms, different investment situations, well they require different valuation measures. It is also worth remembering that companies can distort things. For instance, an investor who only looks at a company's earnings could suffer since firms can distort reported earnings.' Accordingly Bolton uses a range of valuation measures. They range from simple P/E ratios to more complex measures, such as looking at how much cash a company is able to generate after subtracting all the costs it incurs, and looking at how efficiently a firm uses its capital. The particular set of valuation measures he uses varies from company to company.

Balance sheet analysis, the process of investigating a company's financial health based on its published accounts, is undertaken by Fidelity's team of analysts. The firm also subscribes to the services of a number of 'forensic' accountants, whose analyses of company accounts often provide a level of insight and detail that is hard to find elsewhere. Fund managers devote a lot of time to scouring balance sheets since published accounts are complex. Simply looking at headline numbers like pre-tax profits or revenues may not paint an accurate picture about a firm's true worth. More troubling news may be buried in the accounts' detailed figures. 'I'm pretty keen on scouring balance sheets,' Bolton says. 'I learned about the importance of strong balance sheets during the economic recessions of the early 1980s and 1990s – the latter was my worst period. My fund did not

perform well during those recessions, partly because smaller companies with weaker finances struggled in the economic downturn. So
now I pay a lot of attention to balance sheets.'

Bolton never buys a firm's stock unless he or a member of
Fidelity's wider team has met with its management team. 'If a stock
is in the fund, our analysts are obliged to meet or have telephone
contact with its management team every quarter,' he says. 'If the stock
is a big holding, contact will take place more frequently. I can't go to
every meeting – there are too many stocks in my fund for that – so
analysts go on my behalf and give me feedback. However, if it's a big
holding, or an important news item, I'll go myself. If it's developing
differently than we'd expected or hoped, I'll go. If the status quo hasn't
really changed, then I probably won't go. Once we get to know a firm,
we always set the agenda for the meetings. It allows us to focus on
items the management team may not want to, such as a division that
isn't doing well. It also allows me to use a few minutes in the meeting
to ask a firm about its rivals or companies it trades with.'

Next we come to technical analysis, the discipline of analysing share
price charts. Proponents of the technique say the charts reveal repeating patterns you can use to predict future share price movements.
Fidelity has in-house technicians and receives analysis from expert
external technicians, too. Bolton took to using charts very early on in
his career. 'It's one of the things that's stayed with me from my time
at Keyser Ullmann,' he says. 'They employed a technician and I've used
technical analysis ever since. I like to use charts for bigger stocks in particular. I never make an investment decision just on the basis of a
chart, rather I use it as a cross-check of my holdings. It is a cross-check
from a very different angle compared with analysing company
accounts, management teams and so on. It makes you rethink all your
holdings. With bigger stocks I use charts to help me time my investment, to decide how big a bet I should take or to see if we're missing
something. For example, if a chart shows a stock's share price is dete-
riorating, but we like the stock, I will ask an analyst to check it over
again. In essence, charts help me to time investment decisions and to
refine views I've formed based on straightforward company analysis.'

So here we have an anatomy of Anthony Bolton's investment style, one of the most successful ever. It consists of value-based, contrarian investing built on diligent research and detailed analysis. However, there is one last feature of Bolton's approach we have yet to mention, something very hard to describe or replicate. Put simply, it is intuition. Bolton just has a feel for whether a stock is likely to provide a good investment opportunity. 'This is a logic- and evidence-based business,' he says, 'but there is an element of intuition and feel, too. Information goes into the black box inside me and comes out the other side as stocks I want to buy or avoid, and intuition is involved in the process. I can tell you all the things that are important to me, and I can tell you what isn't important to me, but quite how it all blends together – well, I think intuition is involved there.'

Part 2

Special Situations Investing

What exactly is a special situations stock? There is no single answer. Many different types of stock can qualify as a special situation in addition to those favoured by Bolton. For example, some fund managers view firms with a raised chance of making money-spinning discoveries as special situations. Others analyse firms in the throes of litigation if they feel there is a chance the resolution of the dispute will favour one of the litigants. The most that can be said about all these different opportunities is that they resemble each other in the following respect: they are stocks with a raised chance of delivering a significant gain for a specific reason, generally in one or two years' time. This kind of investing is as old as the stockmarket. Investors searched for special situations well before the term, or dedicated special situations funds, were invented.

Modern-day special situations funds usually target unloved small and medium-sized stocks thought likely to rally. This focus on smaller companies makes them sensitive to economic conditions, since smaller firms tend to find an economic downturn tougher to negotiate than larger companies. Consequently, the performance of special situations funds can be volatile, ebbing and flowing with the economic cycle. Moreover, it is hard to say whether an unloved share will enjoy a turnaround in its fortunes. Its price might simply deteriorate. Even if the share does eventually recover, it is hard to predict when that will happen. In the meantime, its price might fall. This makes the stock-picking ability of the person running a special situations fund crucial. A skilled stock-picker is needed to separate the wheat from the chaff. He or she also needs to be courageous enough to stick with their selections if the shares happen to fall in price before recovering. The volatility of special situations funds, the contrarian nature of their investments and their dependence on skilled stock-picking leads many to view them as risky. However, the payoff for shouldering the extra risk is an increased chance of very substantial long-term capital gains, as Bolton's record amply demonstrates.

A good contrast to a special situations fund is provided by a so-called 'core' fund. Core funds are viewed as less risky than special situations funds. They invest in large, mature and well-established companies expected to deliver reasonable rather than spectacular share price growth over the long term. Often the managers in charge of core funds have much less scope to shape their funds' stock portfolios compared with stock-pickers like Bolton. Instead, they work within tight parameters designed to control risk, but which also limit core funds' potential for capital growth. This trade-off between risk and reward is the eternal dilemma investors face. Generally you need to assume greater risk to achieve higher returns. Many fund investors solve the problem by earmarking the majority of their cash for core funds and keeping back a minority for special situations portfolios. If the higher risk special situations funds do well, you profit. If they do poorly, you lose money but keep your shirt, since the majority of your cash is invested in less risky vehicles.

Edward Bonham Carter

The Artful Stock-picker

by Richard Lander

*R*un a fund called Undervalued Assets and you are bound to be
tagged as a value investor looking for cheap shares with bags
of cash or other tangible assets that the market has ignored.
*Edward Bonham Carter doesn't conform to the stereotype. Instead, his
successful fund mixes both classical value shares and growth stocks
that for one reason or another do not trade at their optimal value.*

A True
Value Hunter

I sn't stock-selecting what it is all about? Surely picking the right stocks is the *sine qua non*, or essential requirement, of a success-ful fund manager? Well yes, every successful fund manager does have to end up with a portfolio of stocks that will, over time, outper-form the market. But it is *how* he or she gets there that varies wildly. Only a relatively small minority of top managers, for instance, classify themselves as out-and-out stock-pickers.

Edward Bonham Carter, the joint chief executive of Jupiter Asset Management, falls into this category of stock-pickers, and it is a role he carries out pretty well. Having worked in fund management for more than 20 years, Bonham Carter won the Lipper Citywire All Stars Fund Manager of the Year Award in 2003. He won the gong against tough opposition for the way he had run the £40 million Jupiter Undervalued Assets unit trust, a value stock-picking fund. Delivering an excellent risk-adjusted performance over the three years to December 2002 – perhaps the bloodiest period since the Great Crash – Bonham Carter actually made money for his investors.

So, are stock-pickers different from the rest? Up to a point, says Bonham Carter. Everyone is more or less in the same game. 'I'm a cheapskate trying to buy something for less than £1 that will be worth £1 or more over time. Now, as a mission statement that is slightly misleading because that is what all fund managers are trying to do.' The last thing Bonham Carter wants is to be labelled as one thing or the other. 'I am definitely a value investor, but I find these types of labels as misleading as they are enlightening.'

For one thing, he argues, buying value stocks has been given a bad name by the broad sweeping generalisation that all it involves is picking up lousy stocks – stale crumbs that have fallen off the tables of momentum or growth investors. 'Buying for value doesn't mean buying a bad company. Cheap doesn't necessarily mean good value – just because a share price has gone down doesn't necessarily mean a company is a good investment. The adage that you should invest in a company because it trades at a discount to its book value, has a high yield or is on a low price to earnings ratio doesn't always hold true.'

That said, Bonham Carter is very keen that he gives himself as much chance as possible to run a successful fund while being able to sleep at night. A man with the slight and wiry build of a flat-racing jockey, it seems appropriate that he throws in a gambling metaphor here and there to describe how he reduces risks. 'It's an odds game. Information is imperfect and the market is inefficient, so skill will help you win over time. Markets become more efficient in the medium and long term, but greed and fear are getting more and more influence in the short term.'

Just as no tipster can possibly hope to back the winner in every race, so Bonham Carter accepts from the starting line that not every stock he buys for his fund will end up in the winners' enclosure. 'It's a case of getting more right than wrong. In total, the market is the aggregate of lots of individual and institutional investment decisions. To believe that you can consistently beat it over every time period is either arrogant or foolish,' he argues.

Taking that concept further, Bonham Carter sees his mission as moving the odds in his favour. 'So how can I improve my odds? I

EDWARD BONHAM CARTER: THE MAN

Edward Bonham Carter was born in 1960 and is married with two children. A graduate in Economics from Manchester University, he is a keen, experienced cyclist and enjoys playing chess.

think investing on a value basis can help me because it gives me what Benjamin Graham, the legendary US investor and author of *The Intelligent Investor*, described as a "margin of safety". That means that when you make a mistake your downside is considerably less than that of a growth investor who suffers a double whammy when things go wrong,' he says.

Another odds-gaining strategy for Bonham Carter is to spread the risk among his holdings. 'I don't really like the idea of a focus fund,' he says. In this respect Bonham Carter stands in the tradition of US legendary mutual fund manager Peter Lynch whose giant Magellan fund was spread over more than 1400 stocks. 'I have more than 100 stocks in my own fund – 45% blue chips and 35% small-caps. I like to spread the risk, and small-caps are riskier – less efficiently priced and more illiquid. Too many fund managers place too much emphasis on their own certainty.'

In fact, humility has a big place in the Bonham Carter approach to investing. 'What you need is to have a very nice balance of confidence and self-belief in your own views, but without arrogance and stubbornness,' he says. 'Failure to get this balance right can be fatal, particularly if it means you stick to your investing guns too long. Facts change and you have to change. You have to get that balance plus a sense of humility because the markets have been called the great humiliator with good reason.' The opposite tack will also fail. 'If you're not confident enough you will just replicate consensus and you might as well be a tracker fund.'

Bonham Carter says he also benefits from working alongside other star managers at Jupiter such as Anthony Nutt and Phillip Gibbs. 'I get a lot of feedback from them and I'm a better fund manager for working with these talented managers – we test ideas in the furnace of other good minds.' He compares the process to a star footballer like David Beckham who is a better player for playing alongside other world class players at Real Madrid than he would be if he played for Bolton Wanderers.

Being too stubborn is the main reason, according to Bonham Carter, why apparently all-conquering styles of the past seem to go off the boil as time marches on. He admits that Benjamin Graham's work has been an influence on the way he invests. 'You can't ignore Graham's work, and you have to read Warren Buffett's as well.' He describes the legendary annual reports of Buffett's investment management company Berkshire Hathaway as 'nourishment for the fund management soul'. Bonham Carter also recommends Charles Kindleburger's *Manias, Panics and Crashes: A History of Financial Crises* for the aspiring portfolio manager. 'It is cheap experience – not the same as doing it yourself, mind you, but it is a good place to start.'

However, Bonham Carter avoids thinking of these famous investors as mentors. As he points out, he didn't actually work with them. Ask him to name his biggest influence and he will choose William Littlewood, a former colleague who ran the Income fund at Jupiter in the 1990s before retiring from public investment. 'William had a great instinct for investment – recognising when the market was irrational and taking advantage of that – along with a great sense of the fundamental values of investments'. These qualities are what marked him out for greatness, says Bonham Carter. 'Together they made him a contrarian, and most great investors have that aspect. That's not the same as being contrary, which can be quite dangerous. Part of the skill of being a contrarian is knowing when to go against the crowd and when not to.'

One legacy of working with Littlewood is that it gave Bonham Carter a healthy respect for the influence that top-down macroeconomic factors can have on a share price. Indeed, it is surprising just how much store this renowned stock-picker places on such broad market-moving factors. 'It was a key thing I learned from William – namely that good investing is a combination of top-down and bottom-up. Doing just one of those misses out part of the picture.'

Bonham Carter believes that top-down analysis is very important for a stock-picker to pick out 'which way the river is flowing. You have got to pick out the trend so you can find the right sectors to invest in.'

The traps for ignoring the top-down view of things can be lethal. 'For example, you might spot that UK textile stocks look very cheap but it would be more than useful to know that the sector has been in decline for 100 years or more and is making returns at or below the cost of capital. In other words, it will stay cheap and get cheaper. Top-down analysis helps you answer the question, "Where am I more likely to make a good investment?"'

Underlying Bonham Carter's approach to top-down analysis is a desire to be different from the pack. 'The way I start top-down analysis is to see if the economy is expanding or contracting, and what the outlook is for inflation. That gives you a clue to interest rate movements. You then have to see if your views are different from the consensus, and the results should also point you to certain sectors.'

So far, so conventional. The subtle twist is in realising that conditions change over time while bearing in mind that most investors tend to walk into the same old traps. 'On the one hand, I agree with John Maynard Keynes who said, "If the facts change, change your mind",' says Bonham Carter. 'On the other hand, you have Mark Twain who was famously quoted as saying, "History doesn't repeat itself, but it sure does rhyme."'

Bonham Carter is not saying greed is good – he's far too much of a gentleman to play the red-braced Wall Street investment banker – but greed does play a part at certain defined points, and is there to be taken advantage of. 'Investors' tendencies are usually the same. Towards the end of a cycle investors get excited and greedy and pour

---

CAREER PROFILE

• 1982-1986: Assistant fund manager at Schroder Investment Management.
• 1986-1994: Fund manager of UK and US Equities, Electra Investment Trust.
• 1994-present: Bonham Carter joined the Specialist UK Equity team of Jupiter Asset Management in 1994, was appointed Chief Investment Officer in July 1999 and Joint Chief Executive of Jupiter Asset Management and Jupiter Unit Trust Managers in May 2000. He manages the Jupiter Undervalued Assets fund. He is also Joint Group Chief Executive of Jupiter International Group.

too much money into the market, while companies go out and raise too much money.' The end result is constant. 'The bubble bursts. It has happened often and will happen again – the hardest thing to figure out is when and in what industries.'

But, at heart, Bonham Carter is a stock-picker and believes that choosing the right stocks, rather than being an expert on the economic cycle, is what delivers his great track record. To get this right, he uses dramatic words not often heard in the techno-babble that many fund managers employ today. 'Passion is needed to know about how a company works and what determines its share price. Hunger and curiosity is needed as well because, as Oscar Wilde said, "It is 99 per cent *perspiration* and one per cent *inspiration*."'

What Bonham Carter seeks to do is to make the best interpretation of the facts that are out there about a company. In the Internet age, everybody has the same access to information as the next person. It's what you do with it that makes the difference. In this context, he looks at a company from four perspectives – management, growth, quality and finances.

Investing in good management is not as trite as it sounds, although you never hear a fund manager say, 'I want to invest in bad management', and it is possible to overestimate the influence that management has. Warren Buffett once said that, in the end, business beats management – that is, a good business with bad management is better than the other way around. What Bonham Carter wants to see is managers, especially in smaller companies, who can think like shareholders and demonstrate alignment with their interests. Potential financial pain is a good sign. 'I like to see a significant amount of the managers' wealth invested in the company in real

---

INVESTMENT STYLE

Bonham Carter describes his investment approach as 'bottom-up with a top-down awareness'. That means he looks at the fundamental attributes of individual companies but also takes into account the overall economic conditions for different sectors of the stockmarket.

shares – that's very different from options, which can offer huge upside but at no potential loss.' How great the pain is can be inspired guesswork – we're back to interpretation of the facts. 'Of course, I'm not privy to an individual's wealth because I don't get to see his or her tax returns. But you can get a pretty good idea of what their invest-ment means relative to their wealth, and you can see that one man's £10,000 is equivalent to another man's £1 million.'

He also finds directors' dealings helpful as triggers to buy or sell. 'Directors know more about their companies than outsiders – or at least we hope they do. When you see clusters of directors buying beyond the tax wrapper amount for themselves and spouses, it's a good sign. Selling can be a bit more tricky – it could be to buy a new yacht or to fund a divorce – but again, a cluster can raise a question.'

Management track record is also important. 'Over time you can get a good idea of what they did at previous companies, taking into account what influence they had there and whether they were skilful or just lucky. It's always very important to remember how little we know as fund managers about a sector, so it is very good to talk to managements about what is going on in the market,' he adds, citing the importance of humility again. 'There is a limit to what you can know and understand.'

Assessing a company's growth potential sounds paradoxical for a value manager, but Bonham Carter stands by one inescapable law of

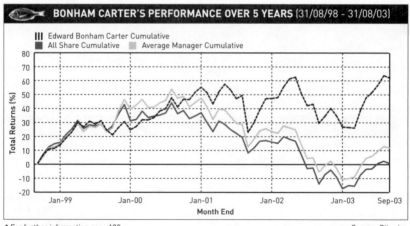

BONHAM CARTER'S PERFORMANCE OVER 5 YEARS (31/08/98 - 31/08/03)

* For further information see p192   Source: Citywire

investment – a company that grows turnover, assets and returns over time will make money for you as an investor. 'Yes, business can shrink profitably but over time you do have to look for growth. So it's important to identify where this growth is going to come from – higher sales, raising prices, and so on.'

For Bonham Carter, the key question is over quality – will the business make a return greater than the cost of capital? Answer that and then ask yourself how long will it be able to do that for, and how big are the barriers to entry, a subject Bonham Carter is very hot on. 'Warren Buffett described businesses as castles, so you need to know how strong the fortifications are,' he says. 'Barriers to entry are tremendously important and would be what I would choose if forced to focus on just one thing. It encapsulates how much growth there is in a business and how sustainable that growth is in the face of competition.'

The notion of quality then spreads out further to take in both customers and suppliers. 'It's worth analysing how strong a company's buying power is to buy the goods and services it needs to run a business as well as its relationship with its customer base,' he says. 'Is it like Tesco – with millions of ordinary consumers on its database of loyal shoppers – or like Rolls-Royce, dealing with just two aircraft makers who, in turn, have a customer base of ailing airlines?'

For Bonham Carter, the synthesis of all this analysis is to see how the first three factors express themselves in numbers, and here he sets great store by a company's cashflow. 'I find that over time cashflow analysis is far more useful than looking at the balance sheet and drawing conclusions from that. Cashflow is a dynamic picture of the business over the full year, whereas a balance sheet is like an X-ray that I may have at the doctor's surgery – it gives a snapshot picture that may be typical or atypical.' He is politely cynical about the value of a balance sheet. 'How can I put it? The balance sheet is "more open to interpretation" in the way it is drawn up, with all sorts of arguments about the value of both tangible and intangible assets.'

But the logic of cashflow for Bonham Carter is very simple. For *him* it shows how the business is converting profits into cash. That, in turn, determines how well it is financing itself and how well it can finance growth in the future without equity dilution or borrowing. 'There is absolutely nothing wrong with employing either of these methods for expansion,' he says. 'But high borrowings leave a company and its investors with less margin for error should things go wrong.'

At this point Bonham Carter tends to swerve from the fine art of interpretation to the more defined science of quantitative data to close the case for investment. 'You still need to find out if there is an investment opportunity there – that's where the scientific analysis comes in. I do find quantitative screens to be very useful but only after having been panning in the river for golden nuggets. At this stage you have to see how the company under scrutiny compares with peers in its sector or in the market as a whole. It may already be priced for perfection,' he says. Nor is Bonham Carter afraid of employing some technical analysis. 'I'm wary of its predictive powers but it is good at showing you where a share price has come from and at helping you question your own prejudices.'

Bonham Carter is adamant that he will only pay the right price for the stocks in his fund – hence the almost exhaustive analysis that goes in to the selection process. 'For me, price is very important. That is the challenge in a low inflation/low growth environment which I believe we are now faced with for some time to come. The task is to find companies that can show genuine growth involving something more than just cost-cutting.'

The result of this right price/no dogma approach is that the Jupiter Undervalued Assets fund sometimes ends up with stocks that look out of place in a value portfolio. At the time of this interview a couple stood out like a sore thumb. One stock, technology developer BTG, even had pride of place once in Bonham Carter's old UK Growth portfolio. Those were the days when, like many a technology stock, it went up in leaps and bounds to £18 ('I still sold it too early,' he says ruefully). Subsequently, Bonham Carter swapped fund horses, and the technology sector sank like a stone. Like old lovers, the two met again. 'BTG came back under £1 and I bought it for value this time – it's got a huge amount of cash and the rest is option money on a host of patents that may pay off.' Within two months of buying the stock, for the second time, it had almost doubled.

It's also hard to see at first glance what place a technology-driven, growth-or-nothing stock such as British Sky Broadcasting has in a value portfolio. 'True, it has a high P/E ratio but it also has a winning business model,' says Bonham Carter. 'The customers like it and it is relatively recession-proof. It's on a par with alcohol and cigarettes [which can be classic value stocks]. People will stop spending on other things before they drop it.'

In the end, it is Bonham Carter's ability to avoid dogma and rules set in concrete that are the keys to his success. He continually questions the value of each share in his portfolio and its right to be there. 'You have to ask yourself why you're holding a share. When I should sell a share is incredibly important – "Have I got anything better to buy with the money? Have the reasons I bought the share changed?" And yes, recognise the limits of what you can and can't do. Maybe when a share price falls it's your own fault – you simply made a mistake!'

Ever the student of human behaviour, Bonham Carter knows it is very hard to admit you made an error and sell at a loss. 'Sometimes you just have to own up and sell.'

Home Truths about Value

The trouble with value-oriented stock-picking is that it brings out the folksy side of supposed investment gurus – people with their own belief systems and superstitions. One value investor will tell you to only invest in companies where the chief executive shares the same canteen and washroom as the staff, while another will warn you never to touch a business where the boss has had a fountain built in front of the headquarters. Some of this advice will inevitably prove right some of the time, but its success will be down to chance alone.

One investor has even admitted to following the example of baseball batboy Eddie Bennett. 'In 1919, at age 19,' he explains, 'Eddie began his work with the Chicago White Sox, who that year went to the World Series. The next year, Eddie switched to the Brooklyn Dodgers, and they, too, won their league title. Our hero, however, smelled trouble. Changing boroughs, he joined the Yankees in 1921, and they promptly won their first pennant in history. Now Eddie settled in, shrewdly seeing what was coming. In the next seven years, the Yankees won five American League titles.' So what does this have to do with management? It's simple – to be a winner, work with winners.

You might think that homage to a bit player in America's national sport is complete nonsense. The only problem is, the investor so influenced by Eddie Bennett is Warren Buffett, the greatest value investor of all time and possibly the most successful investor ever. Born in 1930, Buffett has amassed a net worth of about £20 billion through the simple process of buying stocks trading at a hefty discount to their real value. As one biographer of Buffett put it, 'His approach is simple, even quaint. Ignoring both macroeconomic trends and Wall Street fashions, he looks for undervalued companies with low overhead costs, high growth potential, strong market share and low P/E ratios, and then waits for the rest of the world to catch up.'

If you accused Buffett of diminishing such a complex subject as investment, he probably wouldn't care. For him, investment and life really is that simple. Buffett has always been amazed at the tools young business graduates bring with them when they come to Wall Street: 'Something is taught that is difficult but not useful. The business schools reward complex behaviour more than simple behaviour, but simple behaviour is more effective.'

Just as he eschews all the modern splendours of the markets, ranging from black box investment models to complex derivative instruments ('I view them as time bombs, both for the parties that deal in them and the economic system,' he once said) and 'new paradigm' stocks (he never went near any Internet stocks), so he has turned his back on the supposed necessities of the billionaire class. He lives in the same house he bought in Omaha, Nebraska, for £20,000 four decades ago and regularly dines on burgers and Coke (a typical Buffett stock, which he bought in 1988, when it was on its uppers, and turned into a $13 billion investment).

But even the 'sage of Omaha' had to learn somewhere and Buffett was taught at the knee of someone who has come to be known as the father of value investing, Benjamin Graham. It is thanks to Graham perhaps that so many investors today are numbers-obsessed – it is he who pioneered and popularised the examination of datapoints, ranging from P/E ratios to dividend yields, net current assets and book values. One of his investment strategies – the NCAV (net current asset value) theory – placed very strict criteria on what shares should be bought: 'It always seemed, and still seems, ridiculously simple to say that if one can acquire a diversified group of common stocks at a price less than the applicable net current assets alone – after deducting all prior claims, and counting as zero the fixed and other assets –

the results should be quite satisfactory.'

The only trouble is, as Bonham Carter and others argue, you would end up today with a tiny or non-existent universe of stocks to invest in. So many businesses today are products of intellectual capital that current assets hardly figure on their balance sheets.

That aside, Graham laid a path in 1915 by investing in bankrupt railway stock and making a huge return because he correctly saw that its intrinsic value was worth at least twice its stock price. And it is a path down which Bonham Carter and other top value investors are continuing to walk with huge success today.

Ashton Bradbury

Business Cycle Investing

by Richard Lander

*F*or many fund managers, investment style is everything. Some favour growth, others value. The consequences can be volatile – when the markets turn against them they can find themselves completely out of fashion where once they were flavour of the month. But there is one school of management that refuses to accept this as inevitable. These investors are known as business cycle investors, and their aim is to alter their methods of finding good stocks to invest in according to the state of the market. If they succeed, the result is a style that can attract a following at almost any stage of the market. And Ashton Bradbury's style of investing is attracting followers in ever increasing numbers.

Part 1

A Man for All Seasons

While some fund managers grab the headlines, others prefer to stay in the background. The ones who hog the papers are generally managers who make big decisions quickly. It could be the man who took his small-cap fund into technology stocks just before the sector soared, or the woman who pushed her income fund entirely into bonds the week before the equity market tanked. Managers also make the news when they get things hopelessly wrong, when unit-holders are up in arms, and when they have been stood down by their employers.

Then there are managers such as Ashton Bradbury of Old Mutual Asset Managers (OMAM), whose style is the antithesis of the 'death or glory' school of investing. Bradbury currently heads the top-rated UK Select Smaller Companies fund (he is set to hand over this fund at the end of 2003 to concentrate on the £90 million Old Mutual UK Select Mid Cap fund and the mid/small-cap hedge fund he also heads). For Bradbury and his ilk, the aim is to make the most of what the market has to offer across its entire cycle, not just when it favours one style, say growth, over another, perhaps value. He wants to take a bite of the apple all of the time, not just sit back and go hungry when things go against him. 'I would like to perform well throughout the range of market conditions,' he says. 'My view is that the danger of a highly stylised investment approach is that you almost guarantee to perform poorly in some part of the cycle. You have great growth managers who performed terribly from March 2000 to March 2003, and fantastic value managers who turned in appalling performances between 1997 and 2000.'

The proof is in his record – he has a AAA rating from Citywire and is ranked third over three years amongst the UK smaller companies managers. Bradbury's style of investment is known as 'business cycle investing'. In a nutshell it means changing approach and investment style as the economic cycle progresses. If the good times are set to roll then load up the portfolio with economically sensitive stocks; when economic contraction looms, shift the focus to more defensive companies. It sounds simple and, like many people who do their job well, Bradbury's skill isn't obvious at first. He regards his approach as nothing more or less than common sense – a much-used term in the Bradbury lexicon. 'It is common sense to me to blend top-down and bottom-up analysis for stocks. Very few companies can work outside the business cycle.'

A quiet, softly spoken man, Bradbury is unworried about whether his way of investing was ever celebrated by a famous investment guru or whether it is the subject of intense debate among financial theoreticians. 'Have we looked back 30 years and seen a body of work and decided to invest in that way? Certainly not,' he says. 'We don't really have a label, but if people want to label us then they can call our method business cycle investing. Some people call it rotational investing but that implies rotating the portfolio every month, which we don't do.'

Instead, Bradbury is as Bradbury does. Pin him down to outlining his principles of investing and he will come up with two premises to the way he operates. 'The first is that it is important to vary your approach depending on the type of business you want to buy; the second is that there is no reason why value and growth must be mutually exclusive.' Bradbury has always struggled with the concept of being a 'value investor', the type who wouldn't touch a share if it stands at a premium to the market. 'Why would you not invest in a share trading at a premium if it promised long-term growth of 30% a year? You've got to relate value to what you expect a company to deliver.'

The longer Bradbury talks, the clearer it is that his investment style is not quite as simple as he makes out, and that his diffidence hides a great deal of hard work and intellectual thought. Stating an obvious truth – 'My process comes back to a blend of bottom-up (where the company is going) and top-down' – is much easier than delivering it and knowing how to fine-tune the process.

Balancing the top-down and bottom-up equations is crucial for Bradbury. 'At different points of the cycle the emphasis between top-down and bottom-up changes. At a turning point in the economic cycle you have to place more emphasis on getting the top-down view absolutely right. If, say, we are heading into an economic slowdown, the very worst-run, worst-performing food retailer will probably outperform the very best-run, best-performing steel share.'

Awkwardly, of course, the economy is rarely at such an inflexion point and is usually gradually expanding or contracting. Bradbury thinks investing in the middle of a cycle can be the hardest part of all. 'Here you can get a whole series of industries and sectors performing quite nicely. That is where bottom-up analysis of the companies you are looking at has to add value. You have to pick out and invest in the most attractive stock in each sector to outperform,' he says.

The problem with this combination of top-down and bottom-up analysis is that its proponents have to be experts in both trades, synthesising a set of economic forecasts and fundamentally analysing a universe of stocks that in Bradbury's field of smaller and mid-sized companies can be dauntingly large.

Bradbury has two big assets in his favour, apart from his natural talent and the 15 years of experience he has accumulated since he first helped run a segregated smaller companies fund at a Liverpool stockbroker. First is the five-strong team he runs at OMAM which, as he puts it, 'was chosen in my own mould'. Second is his ability to work incred-

---

ASHTON BRADBURY: THE MAN

Ashton Bradbury was born in 1966, is married with two children and lives in Wales. Bradbury studied Banking and Finance at Loughborough University, where he enjoyed many sports. Still a keen sportsman, he plays reasonable golf, average squash and enjoys fly-fishing. He is also a fan of Leeds United.

ibly hard at absorbing a vast amount of third-party research and developing his own conclusions. Bradbury reads so much, in fact, that there's a case for calling his approach 'head-down' rather than top-down.

The first part of the selection process for Bradbury and his team is the massive output of the City's analytical community. 'We work the same way to come to top-down and bottom-up decisions. We take research from all the major brokers, both sector views for stock selection and strategy pieces for top-down views,' he says. These analysts have not had a great reputation in recent years, especially those looking after companies and sectors. Charges against them include being too close to their subjects, following the pack or being economical with the truth to boost their employer's chances of corporate finance work. However, Bradbury *uses* their work, rather than takes it as gospel, to come to his own conclusions. 'We don't replicate what they do – we have no desire to re-invent the wheel – but we do like to get inside their work and examine the basis of it. In terms of top-down work, we want to understand how individual analysts came up with these numbers, and we question how reasonable that view is from our own perspective.'

Bradbury reckons that's why his view of the UK economy during 2003 gave him a strong advantage. 'At the start of 2003, most economists on the sell side were predicting that UK GDP would grow at about $2^3/_4\%$. We looked at their reports and decided that 2% was about right. We didn't go back to first principles, but we thought they were being too optimistic about consumer spending and international trade. It was a classic example of the way we work.'

The scrutiny process goes even further with the output from company analysts. 'From the bottom-up standpoint, we get the analysts' spreadsheets from their company reports and look at them line by line.' All this extra work is fine and good, but if the work is sub-optimal in the first place, isn't Bradbury and his team building their own analysis on weak foundations? Or, as they say in the information technology business, 'garbage in, garbage out'? Certainly, Bradbury can be critical of much of the work that flows off analysts' desks. He is particularly scathing of the depth of detail in which some of the more scholarly ones immerse themselves when writing a company report. 'When an analyst writes a report that stretches to 100 pages or more there's a huge element of not being able to see the wood for the trees. There's just too much detail and in many cases they have often reached their recommendation conclusion before starting to write the book.'

Bradbury has two further tools of analysis to underscore his approach. The first is to get on the phone to the analyst or meet them to find out what they really think, as opposed to what they are prepared to sign their name to. 'You have to get into a conversation with the analyst, question their assumptions and listen to what they say,' Bradbury says. What comes back is an eye-opener for those who take analysts' reports at face value. 'You then get told things like, "Yes, I do think my forecasts are a bit pushy" or, "I might be able to upgrade a bit later in the year." You find a lot of people who, for whatever reason, don't write what they really mean. You also have the problem of consensus-hugging, where people don't want to stray too far from the pack. We then stress-test these numbers, looking for lack of consistency in the forecasts, to see, for example, if a rise in turnover falls down in the right way to the bottom line.'

Bradbury doesn't just rely on sifting the runes of sell-side analysts' reports. The second tool under his belt is to meet company managements, albeit only on his own terms and in his own City premises. 'We see well in excess of 300 companies a year, the overwhelming number of them in our offices. I differ from most smaller companies fund managers – I really don't see the value of getting out there and kicking the tyres just for the sake of doing it. I will only do it if it really adds value to my understanding, for example by me seeing a brand new technology or a new production technique.'

Bradbury reckons that the fashion to visit a company at its premises is just an excuse for a nice day out of the office. 'You meet up with the company broker at a decent hour and it's all jolly good fun. What you gain I don't really know, and I've certainly never been outside the UK to see a company. A lot of people would say I'm talking rubbish, and good luck to them. All these visits are fine if you are a sector analyst with just 20 companies to cover, but we look at a huge universe of stocks and we can see up to five or six companies here in a day rather than just one at their premises.'

Despite what he thinks, there are few people in the City who think Bradbury talks rubbish, and even fewer who call him work-shy. Indeed, there are few people in the City on any side of the trading divide who work longer hours than Bradbury. Monday to Thursday, he is at his desk more often than not by 7am. 'On a typical day we start off by looking at the news and seeing if there is anything that needs reacting to. Then we will start off with the company visits. I pick and choose mine while the rest of the team go according to the sector they look after. Then we'll be talking to the sell-side analysts.' There's no peace for Bradbury in the evening when he catches up on research reports at his base outside London, but there's a break in routine on Friday when he works from home in south Wales.

Bradbury is keen that the intensive day-to-day routine doesn't cloud the need to take more strategic action to keep the portfolio in shape. 'We hold a weekly meeting to pull together all of the work that we have done during the previous few days and ensure that things are actually done. Then we also have a monthly meeting that is very much a top-down affair. In fact, the participants are not allowed to talk about particular stocks. Instead, they have to look at things from a macro perspective

CAREER PROFILE

- 1988-1991: Charterhouse Tilney, Liverpool
- 1991-1995: Hill Samuel Asset Managers, where he was a member of the smaller companies team.
- 1995-1998: Head of Smaller Companies team, HSBC.
- 1998-2000: Head of UK Smaller Companies then Head of UK Retail, Hill Samuel Asset Managers.
- 2000-present: Old Mutual Asset Managers, where he is currently head of the UK Mid and Small Cap team. He is personally responsible for the Old Mutual UK Select Mid Cap fund and (until the end of 2003) the Old Mutual UK Select Smaller Companies fund. He also runs the Old Mutual UK Specialist Equity Fund Limited, a hedge fund.

Bradbury has a stake in both his smaller companies and mid-cap funds and a few run by other asset management firms, but no direct equity investments in small and mid-cap stocks.

and question what it means for the sectors that they look after.'

He also takes steps to avoid his decisions being driven by information overload. 'There are dangers with my approach to investing. If you're not very careful you can respond to every single element of data and you find yourself swinging around too quickly. You need to have enough experience to avoid that. The risk is that I can be liable to drive my portfolios too hard, wanting to act on something when it is just a little overvalued or undervalued. You have to say to yourself, "Let's wear a little underperformance in the short term to benefit in the long term." It's something I've got to fight against, and it's not an issue you spot when you have less experience.'

With his style of investing mostly free from gurus, Bradbury is hard-pressed to name anybody who has had a huge influence on his professional life. But if there is one person who has steered him in the direction he now follows it is John Ainsworth, an eminent smaller companies investor who was Bradbury's first boss when he moved to London in 1991 and is now his chief executive officer at OMAM. 'He has always believed in the blended approach, standing back from the trends. One thing he said to me has always stuck with me over the years – "There is no point in jumping on the train until you know where the train is going." In the long term, you inevitably pick up things from the person you work for and bring your own bits to that. And I've carried that approach with me wherever I've been and built up teams.'

Bradbury spent four years at Hill Samuel before moving to HSBC, where he set up a new smaller companies team, again using the same methodology. In 1998 Bradbury was on his way back to Hill Samuel to sort out some problems with the smaller companies team. But the return visit was to prove a temporary one. Bradbury chose not to move

---

INVESTMENT STYLE

Bradbury asks three questions of anything he is thinking of buying. Can the business grow faster than the market average over long periods? Is it capable of delivering positive earnings surprises? And is there a chance of it being re-rated?

to Scotland in 2000 when Hill Samuel merged with Scottish Widows under the Lloyds TSB umbrella. Instead he took redundancy. By the autumn of that year he was reunited with Ainsworth.

Bradbury was interviewed for this book at a time of pivotal change for his UK Select Smaller Companies fund, the first significant one since it was launched in 2001. 'Up until this summer [2003] we have been essentially defensive in our mind-set.' That's not to say his team hasn't been on the lookout for attractive growth opportunities. 'You have to look out for how you can implement tactical changes – for example, when things look so oversold you feel sure there will be a bounce. What you have to be clear about in your own mind is whether it was just a tactical bounce or a real shift in sentiment.'

By the summer of 2003 he decided there was a definite shift in sentiment towards growth and decided to switch emphasis in his portfolio accordingly. For Bradbury, however, changes like this are executed steadily rather than with an all-or-nothing approach. 'We tend to roll things gradually to, or away from, economically sensitive areas. I never really want to be in a position where I move one day from having 10% of my fund in housebuilders to having 0% the next. I would much rather move from 10% to 8% to 6%, and so on, over time.'

Bradbury is also prepared to 'stop the clock' in shifting the portfolio if conditions dictate, rather than keep moving the emphasis. 'The great thing about moving things slowly is that you can accelerate or decelerate the process if new evidence comes to light along the way. So, for example, if you get a run of very poor economic data we'll say "Let's halt the roll" and we will start again when things look better.'

At the bottom line, Bradbury and his team give stocks three chances to make a name for themselves in his portfolio. 'We ask three questions about each stock. First, will it grow profits faster than the market for a sustained period? Second, is there a chance the stock will significantly beat market expectations? And finally, is there a chance it will be significantly re-rated by the market?'

Few stocks get ticks in all three boxes but Bradbury's smaller companies fund held two in mid-2003. One was a value stock and the other a growth share, neatly illustrating his agnostic view on which end of the

spectrum his picks come from. As he puts it, 'I feel perfectly confident
with either stock.'

The value stock that ticked all the boxes is Paragon, the buy-to-let
mortgage lender that took a huge leap forward in July 2003 by pur-
chasing the mortgage book of Britannic Money. 'It's a company destined
for double-digit growth, it seems likely to beat market expectations with
huge scope for cost savings and it is starting to be re-rated gradually.'

From the growth end of the spectrum comes Parkman, which
provides outsourcing services to local governments and the Highways
Agency. 'Growth is likely to be about 35-40% in its financial year to July
2004 and 20% the year after. The broker upgrades have started to
happen, giving plenty of potential for Parkman to reach the same P/E
multiples as some of its peers.' Parkman has subsequently merged with
Mouchel, a similar business also offering strong growth prospects.

Simple? Not really – it's just that Bradbury makes it seem that way.

Part 2

Riding the
Cycle

When Ashton Bradbury says there are neither gurus nor gods for his style of investing, he is pretty accurate. True, there are one or two other fund managers in the UK market who follow his method of investing, but they would also be hard-pressed to name anybody who really blazed a trail for them. Still, there is a small body of business cycle investors, principally in the US, who have laid down some of the groundwork, theoretical and practical, for others to follow.

One much-cited study to prove the worth of business cycle investing was carried out by CDA/Weisenberger, an American investment research firm. It compared three strategies – buy and hold, market timing and sector investment – retrospectively over a 10-year period. The buy-and-hold strategy bought and held the S&P 500 index. The market timing technique was defined by correctly predicting price changes in the overall stockmarket of 10% or more in either direction, buying when prices were about to rise and selling when prices were about to decline. And the sector strategy invested the entire portfolio in one of six sectors (energy, financial services, gold, health care, technology or utilities) at the beginning of each year. Each investment strategy started with $1000. At the end of the 10-year period, the buy-and-hold investor's initial investment had grown to more than $6000. By employing the market timing strategy, the nest egg had grown to almost $15,000. But with perfect sector selection, the investment had grown to more than $63,000.

Take note of that word 'retrospectively'. This study did not find the holy grail – it merely provided proof of a concept. 'Remember that the timing and sector strategy results had the benefit of 100% hindsight, which we don't have in the real world,' says Marshall Schield of Schield Management, based in Colorado. 'The significance is in the *potential* return from implementing a sector strategy.'

Schield's firm runs two mutual funds that invest in a range of sector funds. The latter are rather more common in the US than they are in Europe. He chooses sectors using relative strength analysis to gauge how one sector is doing relative to another. Schield says he is looking for 'the dramatic rotation that occurs within these sectors due to economic conditions, political trends, the business cycle, technological developments and demographic trends, etc, that make for investment opportunities.'

This is quite a different application of business cycle investing to the one that Bradbury follows. It is an entirely top-down process in which Schield invests purely in funds to avoid the various misfortunes that can afflict individual stocks – diversification, liquidity and focus. 'Once an attractive industry has been identified,' he says, 'trading individual securities within that favoured industry can be disastrous because the market penalises a company's market price where any earnings disappointment occurs.'

The two Schield funds invest in four and 10 of these sector funds from the 20-strong range run by Rydex Funds (along with Fidelity, this is one of the biggest names in sector funds). In mid-2003, the more aggressive Sector Growth Strategy fund had money spread evenly between retailing, biotechnology, electronics and the money market, while the Sector Total Return Strategy fund had equal positions in those sectors plus leisure, large-cap Europe, financial services, healthcare, technology and utilities.

It is an approach that has worked for Schield (albeit by a less dramatic margin than the retrospective study). The two funds have grown by 128% and 160% respectively since inception in 1993, compared with the 11% gain clocked up by the S&P 500 index.

Another professional inspired by the CDA/Weisenberger study is Sam Stovall, chief investment strategist for ratings agency Standard & Poor's. Having joined the firm in 1989, Stovall was surprised to find that amid all the stock reports S&P had been issuing since evaluating the railroad boom of the 1850s, there was almost no focus at all on individual sectors. To put this right he developed a new publication, *Sector Reports*, in which S&P's teams of analysts projected their industry outlook.

Then came the CDA/Weisenberger study. 'That got me thinking,' says Stovall. 'I had all this data on industry indices, and anybody can find out when economic contractions and expansions started and ended, so I decided to determine what sectors performed the best during different periods of an economic cycle.'

Stovall's number-crunching involved sorting the economic cycle into five phases (early, middle and late expansion followed by early and late contraction) and then seeing which industry sectors outperformed the market at which stages.

The key datapoint that he developed was what he called a 'batting average' – a figure indicating how often sectors outperform throughout the cycle. Certain sectors with high averages (broadcast media, household products and tobacco) did well throughout the cycle, while others, such as airlines and automobiles, only prospered in certain phases.

Like Schield, Stovall is a student of sector-relative strength but goes further and does some number-crunching from a bottom-up basis as well. 'I also have the P/E ratio, relative P/E, indicated dividend yield and then their 25-year average to decide whether it's high or low based on the average,' he says.

He is also well aware that history may be a great guide but it is no guarantee to the future. In this respect he is like Bradbury, insisting that you have to have a deep understanding of an individual company to see where it might be going.

Stovall's early industry sector studies were made just after the Berlin Wall came down and the geo-political map of the world shifted permanently. So while his studies showed that the aerospace sector had outperformed four out of four times in the first third of an economic expansion and underperformed in all succeeding phases of the expansion and contraction, all bets were off in a world that needed a different type of defence strategy.

It is little wonder that the legions of business cycle investors are small but of high quality. From macroeconomic policy to interest rates and consumer sentiment on the one hand, to company management style and balance sheet analysis on the other, there is scarcely a metric or fundamental factor that is disqualified from being included in this style of investing.

Kent Shepherd
Thinking Big

by Sunil Jagtiani

*L*arge companies dominate the world of investment. Pick any well-known stockmarket from around the world and you will probably find that shares in large companies account for the majority of its value. In both the UK and US, for example, the value of large stocks runs into the trillions and is only a little short of the entire value of each country's stockmarket. Equally, funds investing in large stocks dominate the mutual fund industry. Most people who put money into the stockmarket tend to have a fair bit of their cash invested in large stocks, whether directly or through funds. This chapter examines the investment techniques of Kent Shepherd, a seasoned large stock investor who works for US firm Franklin Advisors, before going on to look at large stocks in general.

Part 1

The Contrarian

K ent Shepherd, Senior Vice President of US investment house Franklin Advisors, has the rare and perhaps unfortunate distinction of having once worked for a firm destroyed by a notorious financial scandal. The company in question was Drexel Burnham Lambert, which in the 1980s created and became the most important player in the high-yield or 'junk' bond market. The development of the high-yield market revolutionised corporate America, enabling firms to raise capital quickly and relatively easily by issuing junk bonds to investors rather than relying on bank loans. Some academics say this new source of finance substantially increased the US economy's potential because it enabled firms to grow rapidly. However, despite its pioneering role in changing the US economy permanently, Drexel folded after its star trader, Michael Milken, became embroiled in an insider trading scandal. Regulators fined Drexel $650 million in 1988, and by 1990 it was bankrupt. Milken was hit with a $200 million fine and served 22 months in jail.

Shepherd was a recently graduated 22-year-old when he joined Drexel. He worked there for three years in junior positions then left for business school before the firm's darkest final days. Nevertheless, as you might expect, his experiences and the company's collapse left a mark on him. 'Working for Drexel was a fantastic introduction to Wall Street and the US financial markets in general for a fresh-faced 22-year-old,' Shepherd says. 'But let's just say my experiences left me with a healthy general scepticism towards Wall Street. Now don't get me wrong, Wall Street provides a way for firms to raise capital and is invaluable to America's free-market economy. It also includes in its ranks many talented and upstanding people. But I believe it is crucial to properly understand what makes Wall Street tick. Secondly, my time at Drexel taught me to avoid arrogance, since I believe the firm became arrogant given its domination of the high-yield bond market. This left it with no friends among Wall Street's elite in its final days, friends it desperately needed. Watching Drexel struggle and ultimately collapse was a very vivid lesson in how *not* to behave when things are going especially well. Thirdly, my experience at Drexel taught me that it can be very, very dangerous to work for, or invest in, firms with poor ethical leadership. However, on a more positive note, I also learned that great things can be achieved in a meritocracy that encourages truly independent thinking. Challenge consensus thinking, and don't get sucked into seeing things the same way everyone else sees them. That concept has helped me a great deal as an investment manager.'

Shepherd joined Franklin Advisors in 1991 after completing extensive postgraduate business studies. The firm, which manages about $26 billion worth of assets, is a subsidiary of Franklin Resources, also known as Franklin Templeton Investments, a $12 billion company listed on America's S&P 500 index. Shepherd heads up Franklin Advisors' large-stock investment team from its sprawling headquarters on the outskirts of San Francisco, California. He runs a number of funds, whose combined assets total $2 billion, for both private and institutional investors. The largest fund he runs for retail investors is the $700 million Franklin US Equity fund. He took charge of the port-

⬲ KENT SHEPHERD: THE MAN

Kent Shepherd was born 1964 and is married with three children. He has a BA in Economics and Political Science from Northwestern University, and an MBA in International Finance from the University of California, Los Angeles. He loves outdoor activities.

folio in January 2000, a little before the stockmarket reached its peak and then crashed. The fund is down 8.77% since then, much better than the 24% fall in the S&P 500 index over the same period. Shepherd managed to avoid big losses between 2000 and the first few months of 2003, a fate that befell many of his rivals during one of the toughest periods in the history of the stockmarket. It is also worth noting that Franklin US Equity had assets of just $9 million when Shepherd took charge of it. The fund attracted a large amount of extra cash thanks to the performance record he established.

As befits an employee of Franklin Templeton Investments, Shepherd cites one of the firm's progenitors, Sir John Templeton, as a major influence on his career. Sir John has attained legendary status for his performance as a fund manager, businessmen and philanthropist. In 1939, on the eve of the Second World War when he was just 26, Sir John borrowed $10,000 to buy 100 shares in each of the 104 companies selling at one dollar or less on the New York stockmarket. Few other investors at the time wanted much to do with the stockmarket. Moreover, some 34 of the firms Sir John backed were bankrupt. Yet only four of the investments turned out to be worthless. The rest delivered large profits on average four years later. Sir John is renowned, too, for investing heavily in Japan in the early 1960s, an unfashionable move at the time but one that led to big profits when the Japanese stockmarket took off.

Sir John built up an investment management firm, Templeton, Galbraith & Hansberger, whose best-known fund was Templeton Growth. The fund, launched in 1954 and run by Sir John for nearly three decades, retains its fame because of its investment record. A $10,000 investment put into the fund at launch – admittedly a princely sum at the time – would now be worth more than $4 million.

CAREER PROFILE

- 1986-1989: Drexel Burnham Lambert.
- 1991-current: Franklin Advisers. Now Senior Vice President, the fund that made Shepherd's name, and which he still runs, is the Franklin US Equity fund.

Sir John sold Templeton, Galbraith & Hansberger for $440 million in 1992 to Franklin Resources. After he quit the investment business he went on to manage the John Templeton Foundation, which gives about $40 million a year to various causes. In 2003 he was rated the 68th richest Briton in *The Sunday Times* Rich List, which estimated Sir John's fortune at £450 million.

Given all these achievements, it is hardly surprising that Sir John's career and fund management skills have made such a big impression on Shepherd. 'Sir John is now commonly referred to as one of the great value investors with a unique ability to spot attractively priced stocks,' Shepherd says. 'And yet the longest standing fund at Templeton is Templeton Growth, which he launched and ran for so many years! This shows that you have to be careful not to make too much of the distinction between value and growth investing. What I like about Sir John is his independence of thought, the rigour with which he analysed stocks and his willingness to take a hit in the short term in order to make the right long-term calls. He was prepared to take a different view from the consensus and that, in my opinion, is critical to successful investing. 'The second major influence on me has been Charlie Johnson, our chief executive officer. As an investor he, too, is an extremely courageous contrarian. He recognises that you need the confidence to have a different point of view.'

Shepherd's approach to managing his large company funds begins with a statement of his basic purpose. 'We view ourselves as being in one core business,' he says, 'which is finding mis-priced stocks. That is, we make a judgement about what we think a company is worth, which is no easy task. We then compare our judgement with the company's share price, to see if the shares are trading above, below or in line with what we think they are worth. That is really the most critical assessment we make, which determines if we succeed or fail.

INVESTMENT STYLE

Shepherd is a large-cap value investor with a contrarian streak who likes to think independently.

One point I want to stress is that we're stock-pickers. We start by analysing firms to see if they present attractive opportunities. Of course we need to try to understand the economic, industrial, technological and regulatory environment, but our major focus is on analysing companies. Some fund managers focus more on general trends and work downwards to find investments. For example, they will observe that the US population is ageing, which suggests that drug consumption should increase. This in turn implies that the pharmaceutical sector is a good place to invest. So they will try to find pharmaceutical companies to back. Normally, we don't work that way – our focus is to analyse companies, not "big picture" trends, to uncover investment opportunities.'

Shepherd finds his stock picks by examining companies in the S&P 500 index, so named because it is made up of America's 500 leading firms. He and a team of 41 other analysts and fund managers undertake the gruelling task of company analysis. Members of the team meet each week to review investments and discuss new ideas. 'We go through a template of issues at the meeting,' Shepherd says. 'For example, we will look at how successfully a firm is competing compared to rivals in its industry, the quality of its senior management team, its accounts and its valuation. But it should be noted that different companies lend themselves to different means of analysis. So, in the course of our analysis we will look at a whole host of valuation measures.'

Apart from the erstwhile P/E ratio, other key valuation measures used by Shepherd and his team include the price-to-book and return-on-equity ratios. Assessments linked to a firm's enterprise value are also important. The price-to-book ratio compares a firm's stockmarket value with its assets, while the return-on-equity ratio compares a firm's profit levels with its assets. The enterprise value of a company basically tells you what it would cost to acquire the business. All these measures enable Shepherd and his team to refine their judgement as to whether a stock is attractive or not. 'Really we want to focus on the most relevant valuation measure for the company in question,' Shepherd says. 'Our job is to assess a company's fair worth and to see to what extent that is reflected in the firm's share price.'

Deploying this approach to identify winning large company stocks is no easy task. In fact, many professional investors argue that running a large company fund successfully is one of the toughest tasks in the fund management industry. They say so because large stocks are very well researched by thousands of dedicated analysts and media commentators. Such wide coverage suggests that if a large company's shares are mis-priced and present an investment opportunity, stock buyers will soon come to know about it. They will buy the firm's shares, driving up its share price and eliminating the opportunity. Shepherd agrees with this view to an extent. But he argues that large company investors are prone to forming a consensus view about a stock. This 'herd mentality' can be strong enough to make them dismiss information that runs counter to the consensus, even if the information suggests that a stock presents an investment opportunity because it is mis-priced. Eventually, the herd will turn and recognise the opportunity, but until then fund managers who move early can position themselves to benefit from the stampede. However, you need to be a brave fund manager to use this tactic, since moving early entails buying an out-of-favour stock whose price may continue to slide. The payoff will come if and when the stock's fortunes turn, but until then you need the courage of your convictions.

'A large company is created over time because it profitably produces a good or a service in great demand,' Shepherd says. 'By the time it has a become a large company, the firm has already won over a big constituency of supporters and has probably been analysed very thoroughly. This means that the potential for consensus-thinking about the stock is greater. So, while I do agree to an extent with those who say it's tougher for large company fund managers to perform well, nevertheless the greater coverage of large company stocks increases the potential for herd-thinking. That's why I think it's extremely important to maintain an independent view. You shouldn't be afraid of owning more or less of a stock than everybody else. You must be willing to step away from the crowd. You need diligent independence, as opposed to following Wall Street or convention, to find mis-priced assets. It's a hard thing to do, and you have to be patient – we're willing to wait for the right opportunity to come along, and to wait two to three years for one of our investments to achieve what we think it can. Sometimes there may be a temporary circumstance we can exploit, but generally we make mid- to long-term investments. I never know exactly how long it will take for an investment to come good when I first make it.'

Shepherd can point to a number of examples where his funds have benefited from independent, contrarian thinking. Some of the most interesting stem from the year 2000, just before the bubble in technology, media and telecoms (TMT) stocks burst. Shepherd and his team felt that a number of technology stocks had become far too expensive. Moreover, they believed the phenomenon was so pronounced and significant as to suggest that a major stockmarket correction was on the way. Yet, at the time, technology stocks of any flavour were incredibly popular, while proponents of the view that the market was set for a big correction were in the minority. So when Shepherd and his team started dumping technology stocks, in preference for out-of-favour, even boring non-technology companies, they were acting against the consensus. 'We were looking for a place to survive the impending storm,' Shepherd says. 'Though we didn't know exactly when it was going to happen, we knew something was going

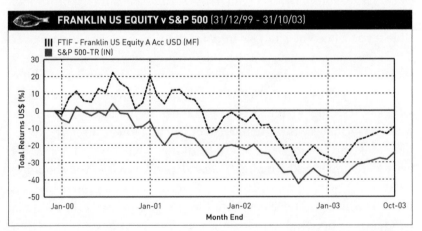

Source: Lipper

to happen. We felt there was a high chance it was on the way. So we searched for under-priced stocks. Subsequently, we moved a signifi- cant slice of the fund into stocks that were growing less rapidly and viewed as unexciting. They were out of favour and cheap. It turned out to be the right way to go. Once the storm hit, investors quickly traded 'sexy' technology stocks for less exciting but more stable non- technology shares.'

One example of this strategy in action is provided by Proctor & Gamble, an investment Shepherd feels typifies his approach to fund management. The firm manufactures a host of household brands known to many millions the world over. 'For many years Proctor & Gamble was viewed as a beloved growth story among larger compa- nies,' Shepherd says. 'It didn't have the highest growth levels in the market, but everyone just felt it would grow at a reasonable pace forever. Then along came the incredible stockmarket bubble in tech- nology stocks, which diverted people away from slow, dependable growth stories. The firm also posted a few disappointing results for a variety of reasons, like a strong dollar, increased competition and changes in its senior management. So investors formed the view that Proctor & Gamble had lost its magic touch.' In fact, the change in sen- timent was so sharp that the firm's share price tumbled from nearly 120 cents in January 2000 to the low 50s by March of the same year. If you draw a graph of the slide you have to plot an eye-catching, near-vertical drop.

'We initiated a position in Proctor & Gamble literally after the big fall and it became one of our largest investments,' Shepherd says. 'If I remember rightly we picked up the stock when its price was in the low 60s. Of course, it hadn't hit rock bottom then – it fell a bit more to the 50s. As a result we bought some more. We felt the stock was extremely oversold. The crucial factor in our decision was Proctor & Gamble's P/E valuation. Historically, the stock had traded at a P/E of over 30 on a steady basis for a number years. Yet the P/E fell to 18 fol- lowing the tumble in the firm's share price. Now, a P/E of 18 isn't the cheapest in the world, but relative to its traditional valuation, its peers and the stockmarket, it looked good. The stock went on to perform extremely well for us.' In fact, Proctor & Gamble's share price rose above 90 cents by March 2002, a gain of about 75% from its March 2000 low.

Data storage firm EMC provides another good example of Shepherd's contrarian approach to picking large company stocks. But, unlike Proctor & Gamble, it is an example of a well-timed sell rather than buy. 'EMC was the number one performing stock in the S&P 500 from 1995 to 2000, rising an astounding 3000% during the period,' Shepherd says. 'It was one of the first companies to recognise the explosive growth in demand for data storage products, and was the first to roll out a comprehensive data storage solution. Our technology team spotted the company's potential early. We bought the stock in the mid-$20s and sold in the mid-$70s early in 2000, more than tripling our money. Now, the stock rose towards $100 later in the year and, of course, I kicked myself as it did so. But fundamentally we had to make a judgement about the long-term fair worth of the company, and to compare that with the stock's current share price. Could EMC replicate the past and continue to be the dominant player in the data storage sector? Or would powerful new entrants such as IBM, Sun, Dell and Compaq take some of the action? Well, as we expected, the latter happened. EMC was still a great company, but we felt its share price and valuation had risen to levels implying unrealistic growth expectations. And by the second half of 2001 its share price had fallen to below the price we'd paid to buy the stock. So EMC is an example of the critical judgements we have to make about a larger company's future prospects.'

Shepherd, of course, is not the only fund manager to practise a contrarian investment strategy. Many professional investors describe themselves as contrarians who buy unloved but cheap stocks and sell popular but expensive ones. It is a strategy they hope will enable them to 'buy low and sell high'. Yet private investors perennially make the mistake of buying high and selling low, as many did to their great cost during the TMT bubble. The problem they face is that the contrarian approach requires a lot of courage. It involves buying a stock when all around are telling you to avoid it, or selling a stock at a time when it is popular. In the former case, the stock price may continue to slide before it improves. In the latter scenario, it may rise higher than the price you sold at before falling back. If you lack the confidence to sustain short-term losses or to miss out on short-term gains in the interest of long-term success, you will probably chicken out of the contrarian strategy. 'If you haven't got the fortitude, if you're going to panic, it won't work for you,' Shepherd concludes. 'To be a successful contrarian you have to be willing to be wrong to be right.'

The Dominance of Large Companies

Take a cursory look at the mutual fund industry on either side of the Atlantic and you'll soon see it is dominated by funds investing in big firms with large stockmarket capitalisations, or 'large-caps' for short. Funds dedicated to mid-sized or small stocks are much less prevalent. The story behind why this is so is a complex one. But, in essence, the amount of money committed to the stockmarket by private and corporate investors rose greatly during the 1980s and 1990s. The easiest way for fund managers to look after such large sums was to invest in large-caps, because big firms' shares can be traded in large quantities relatively easily. The result is a modern mutual fund industry dominated by large-cap funds. Of course, this extra demand for large-cap shares pushed up their price. The price rises in turn attracted yet more investors, stoking demand for large-caps. A cycle was established whereby the market value of large-cap shares rose greatly through the 1980s and especially the 1990s.

Today, large-caps dominate the stockmarket. Take the FTSE 100 index of the UK's 100 largest stocks as measured by their market capitalisation. These 100 stocks, which include household names such as Vodafone and BP, are worth about £1 trillion. Meanwhile, the FTSE All Share index, which includes the 100 largest firms together with 587 other medium-sized and small stocks, has a value of £1.2 trillion. This means the 100 largest stocks account for more than 80% of the capitalisation of the FTSE All Share's 693 stocks. The US stockmarket tells a similar story. The 500 firms in its main index of large companies, the S&P 500, which includes giant organisations such as General Electric and Microsoft, are worth about $9 trillion altogether. The S&P SuperComposite 1500, which is made up of these 500 firms together with 400 medium-sized and 600 small stocks, has a market capitalisation of just over $10 trillion. So, the leading 500 stocks account for about 90% of the SuperComposite 1500 in terms of stockmarket value.

In general, there are two types of large-cap funds investors can choose from: so-called passive index-tracking funds and actively managed funds. Passive index-tracking funds simply aim to replicate the make-up of a large-cap stock index, such as the S&P 500 or the FTSE 100. The return you get if you invest in these funds will be the return achieved by the index they track, less fund charges. Take the S&P 500 and one of the funds that tracks it, the Vanguard 500. The fund happens to be the world's biggest, with assets of $83 billion. Each of the stocks in the S&P 500 has a particular weighting, reflecting its market value – the bigger the value, the bigger the weighting. In mid-2003, the five companies with the biggest weightings in the S&P 500, in descending order, were General Electric, Microsoft, Pfizer, ExxonMobil and Wal-Mart Stores. Similarly, the Vanguard 500's top five holdings comprised the same stocks. Their weighting in the fund matched their weighting in the index. General Electric, for example, had a weighting of about 3.2% in the index, and so accounted for 3.2% of the Vanguard 500's assets. The return the fund's investors get is determined by the index's fortunes, rather than the skill of a fund manager busily deciding which of the 500 stocks to buy or sell. About $1 trillion is indexed to the S&P 500. There are well over 100 S&P 500 trackers to choose from in the US alone, never mind funds that track other large-cap indices, such as the Dow Jones Industrial Average.

The alternative to an index tracker is an actively managed large-cap fund, whose performance is down to the skill of the man or woman running it. There are thousands of actively managed large-cap funds in the US, and many others in other fund centres such as the UK. We can take Kent Shepherd's Franklin US Equity fund as a typical example. It aims to beat the performance delivered by the S&P 500.

It tends to own about 100 stocks gleaned from the index, rather than all the index's 500 stocks, as in an index tracker. Moreover, Shepherd will often give the stocks in his fund a very different weighting compared with their index weighting. For example, in mid-2003 the fund's top five holdings were Pfizer, Microsoft, PMI Group, American International and Amerisourcebergen, quite different to the top five stocks in the S&P 500 as detailed earlier. So far, Shepherd's stock-picking ability has delivered markedly better returns than the S&P 500 index, based on Franklin US Equity's performance since he took charge of the fund in January 2000.

Debate continues to rage over which type of fund – active or passive – provides the best way to gain exposure to large-cap stocks. One school of thought says that over the long term active managers cannot beat a large-cap index. Consequently, investors are better off putting their money into a passive index-tracking fund, which typically charges much lower fees than an actively managed fund. This view is based on a complex academic theory – the 'efficient market hypothesis' – developed in the late 1960s and early 1970s by Eugene Fama, who today is a finance professor at Chicago University. Stripped down, the theory suggests that stockmarkets reflect all the information available about individual stocks and the stockmarket as a whole very efficiently. If new information arises that a stock is mis-priced and presents an investment opportunity, the information will feed into the stockmarket rapidly. The stock's price will adjust quickly and the opportunity closes. Of course, you cannot know the new information before it emerges. If you cannot know that, you cannot know what will happen to the stock's share price, which means future stock price movements are unpredictable and random. Putting all this together, if existing large-cap share prices are fair value because they reflect all the available information, and future investment opportunities are unpredictable and fleeting, it would seem that active fund managers who aim to beat the stockmarket over the long term face the toughest of tasks. So, rather than paying high charges to a fund manager who in all likelihood cannot beat the stockmarket, buy a much cheaper index-tracking fund to achieve the stockmarket's rate of return.

As you might expect, this a hotly disputed argument. After all, stock prices are not simply a rational function of publicly available information. They are also a function of the psychology and behaviour of investors. The latter is far from rational, and appears to lead to clear cases of mis-pricing, as the stockmarket bubble in TMT stocks of late 1999 and early 2000 appears to demonstrate. This is what Kent Shepherd referred to in the first part of this chapter when he said large-cap investors were prone to a herd mentality, which he argued gave him the opportunity to beat the stockmarket by deploying a contrarian investment strategy. Of course, we cannot hope to adjudicate on the debate between proponents and opponents of the efficient market theory here. It is an argument that is likely to keep academics in tenure for decades to come. Proponents say fund managers who consistently beat the market are lucky, while opponents say stock-picking skills are involved. The issue, of course, cuts to the heart of this book – are the managers featured here very lucky or very skilled? No-one can say for sure, but common sense suggests both luck and judgement are involved.

Harry Nimmo
Small is Beautiful

by Sunil Jagtiani

*I*nvesting directly in smaller companies is a popular pastime for private investors. They hope to make money by spotting a few undiscovered gems that grow in size and thereby deliver healthy share price gains. The opportunity is said to arise from the fact that many of the stockmarket's biggest professional investors tend to avoid smaller companies. These professionals prefer to focus on large stocks because they are well researched by analysts and can be traded easily in substantial quantities. Private investors with the confidence to deal in small-cap shares directly hope to capitalise on the professionals' over-sight. Ideally, they want to find a winning minnow that becomes big enough to interest the professionals. Fund managers in charge of smaller company funds do the same. They often use trite but accurate sound-bites to sum up what they do, for example 'buying tomorrow's larger companies today'. Most also describe themselves as growth investors.

The first part of this chapter examines the distinctive investment techniques of one such fund manager, Scotsman Harry Nimmo. A land surveyor turned stock-picker, Nimmo has become one of the UK's leading smaller company investors. The second part of the chapter looks at the role small stocks play in investment portfolios, and questions whether small stocks deliver better returns than the stockmarket as a whole over the long term.

Nimmo's Small Stock System

H arry Nimmo has managed Standard Life's £75 million UK Smaller Companies fund since its launch in January 1997. He works for Standard Life Investments at its headquarters in Edinburgh. The firm is a subsidiary of Standard Life Group, an insurer and investment manager with £83 billion under management. Nimmo joined in 1985 after completing an MBA at Edinburgh University, having spent the first part of his career as a map-maker in Saudi Arabia. The switch from cartography to fund management looks a very surprising one at first glance. Nimmo's family history sheds some light on the matter. His father was a keen private investor, and this sparked his son's interest in the stockmarket. 'My father would keep up to 100% of his spare cash in equities,' he says. 'The only time he ever mentioned the stockmarket with a furrowed brow was during the 1973-1974 crash caused by the Middle East oil embargo. He said, "It's a nightmare out there, we'll have to tighten our belts", but he stuck with it. When I worked abroad in Saudi Arabia in the early 1980s I'd get paid every month in cash, a large wedge of small denomination notes, and I'd send some home and we'd put it in shares. So I always had an interest.'

Nimmo's first stint at Standard Life Investments was as a US equities analyst. He moved to the UK large-cap team in 1990 and three years later found his permanent home as a manager of smaller company funds. His tenure as lead manager of Standard Life UK

Smaller Companies stretches over 7 years. The fund has performed significantly better than many of its rivals for most of this period, and is well ahead of the smaller company stockmarket. A £1000 investment into the fund at launch in January 1997 is now worth £1590. On average, rival funds have turned £1000 into £1160, while the rise in the small-cap stockmarket has added £110 to the original figure. Nimmo says he aims for a long-term performance record that puts Standard Life UK Smaller Companies in the top 25% of all UK smaller company funds, which in mutual fund jargon is known as 'top quartile' performance. It may seem odd that Nimmo should aim for the top 25% rather than first place, but aiming for first place often requires taking more risk. Nimmo prefers a steadier, lower-risk approach for more modest but consistent, healthy gains.

His fund management style is distinctively rigorous and systematic. It comprises a three-stage investment process in which he sets out his objectives, screens the stockmarket for investment opportunities and then researches the firms highlighted by the screening process thoroughly. Each of these steps is described in more detail later. Nimmo set out this well-defined approach in 1995, two years before he launched Standard Life UK Smaller Companies, and applies it religiously. 'I say what the investment process is and I stick to it,' Nimmo says. 'I don't want investors to get nasty surprises down the line. The fund's performance should always be explainable. I'm incredibly suspicious of fund managers who say, "Trust me, it's all up here in my head – I'm incredibly intelligent and that's what makes me a good investor, though I can't tell you much about my investment process." I prefer to spell out my process, and I'm careful about risk. From us you get top quartile performance over the medium to long

HARRY NIMMO: THE MAN

Harry Nimmo was born in 1957 and is married with three children. He graduated with an MA in Geography from Dundee University and, a year later, in 1980, was awarded a Diploma in Surveying from Glasgow University. He loves hill-walking and playing squash.

term but for below-average risk. After all, smaller company investing is an arena fraught with danger for the gullible. If you get it wrong you can easily see your investments halve in value quickly.'

The first stage of the investment process, cryptically called 'top level guidelines', in essence sets out his overall aims. 'I like to think we're buying tomorrow's larger companies today,' Nimmo explains. 'That's a mantra for me. I like companies that can go all the way, from £50 million to £1 billion. These aren't very common but there have been a few. I don't buy bombed-out stocks where there might be a recovery or a quick turnaround. I like to get stocks I can hold for a number of years. I also like companies that operate in a growing market and I like firms that make money.' Nimmo adds that his focus on profitable companies 'kept him out of danger' during the boom in technology stocks in late 1999 and early 2000. In contrast, many investors who backed newly floated technology firms with little or no revenues, let alone profits, suffered badly in the long bear market that followed the boom.

The second stage of Nimmo's investment process consists of a stock selection matrix that evaluates a potential investment against a number of factors. The matrix was developed in the first instance on the UK desk at Standard Life. Stocks go through it and get a score depending on how well they do. The first factor in the model is whether analysts are upgrading their forecast for a company's earnings. Many fund managers believe such companies are best placed to deliver rising share prices. The second variable is the extent to which a company's directors are buying or selling its shares. Clearly, if the people running a business like or dislike its shares at a particular time, outside investors are bound to take note. The matrix also looks at the trend in a company's share price, on the assumption that a rising share price is better than a sliding one. Fourthly, the model uses standard techniques to value a stock, such as P/E ratios and dividend levels. The final two factors look at whether a company is in danger of going bust, and at who else owns its stock. If research reveals that fewer people or firms own a stock than you might expect given the quality of the business, there is a chance its share price will rise as more investors take note.

Nimmo argues each of these factors help to indicate the likely direction of a share price. 'We've tested them using historic share price movements and we feel the matrix works,' he says. 'We tend to be buyers of shares with higher matrix scores. If the score is more than 10, I tend to be a buyer, whereas if the score is -10, and the stock is in my fund, I'm looking to sell. The stock needs to emerge with a score of 10 or more before I go on to research the company in detail.' The matrix is held in a spreadsheet and updated daily by the team of analysts and fund managers who work alongside Nimmo. It represents, arguably, the most systematic approach to screening small-cap stocks of any UK smaller company fund manager.

Once the stock matrix has highlighted investment opportunities, Nimmo's next step is to test for false positives. This entails researching a company thoroughly to determine whether it is a genuinely attractive investment or a rogue result mistakenly churned out by the stock selection matrix. Again, Nimmo's investment process breaks down this kind of company analysis into a number of clear steps. The most important is meeting the management team in charge of a firm, usually the chief executive and finance director. 'There are an awful lot of charlatans out there,' Nimmo warns. 'Some managers and directors can present very well and have a very bad business, while others have a great business but present very poorly. Over time you develop a relationship with directors, which is both a good and a bad thing. It's good because you get to know the business very well, but it's bad because you must guard against falling in love with a firm too much. One of the ways I can do the latter is through the results of the stock selection matrix.'

Aside from meeting management teams, Nimmo speaks to company analysts within and outside Standard Life Investments. The information he gleans helps him to work out whether a firm operates in a favourable industry and has made the most of its advantageous circumstances. In particular, Nimmo looks to see whether an industry is growing and has 'barriers to entry' that discourage firms from entering it. The more barriers there are, the better, since they protect existing companies in the industry from new sources of competition.

Nimmo also searches for 'pricing power', another industry feature he feels is very important. Pricing power refers to the freedom firms in an industry have both to charge healthy prices and to raise their prices over time. Some industries are very competitive and offer little pricing power, which makes it difficult for the firms they house to make profits. In contrast, an industry with pricing power should contain profitable companies that are attractive to investors.

Once Nimmo and his team members have analysed a firm's industry sector, they need to satisfy themselves that the company has a high and possibly growing share of its market. 'Barriers to entry, pricing power and market share – we need to find evidence of these factors before we include a firm in the fund,' Nimmo says. Next, the team looks at the level of dividends a firm pays its shareholders. A company able to fund rising dividends from increased earnings is particularly attractive. This is because the firm's ability to do so provides evidence that its business concept and strategy are both sound. Finally, Nimmo looks at a firm's culture, one of the hardest things to assess unless you work at a firm. Two factors help him assess a firm's culture: whether its staff own shares in the company, and the level of staff turnover. Ideally, a firm should tie-in its staff by giving them more shares the longer they stay. Such a situation would augur well for the company's future. In contrast, a firm suffering from frequent staff changes, with share ownership skewed in favour of a few people at the top, will probably be less attractive to investors.

The result of all this analysis is a fund with about 55 carefully scrutinised holdings. This contrasts with other smaller company fund managers who sometimes invest in hundreds of stocks. 'I call my

---

CAREER PROFILE

- 1980-1984: Land Surveyor and Survey Controller for Al Jalahima & Al Amoudi & Co, Dammam, Saudi Arabia.
- 1984-1985: MBA from Edinburgh University.
- 1985-present: Fund manager with Standard Life Investments. He currently runs the Standard Life UK Smaller Companies fund, the fund that made his name and which he also invests in.

fund a conviction-led portfolio,' Nimmo says. 'I'd say 98% of my stocks are in the fund because I want them to be in there. The remaining 2% are stocks I'm in the process of selling. There aren't as many stocks in the tail end of the fund as you might find elsewhere. I don't like having a long tail of duffers. This is all part of my systematic approach to fund management. My aim is to be rigorous and sensitive to risk. I look at the stock selection matrix every day and I won't move on a stock until I get a steer from the screening process.'

In fact, Nimmo's rigorous techniques reflect some of the more important influences on his fund management style. Two books, in particular, have shaped his thinking – *What Works On Wall Street* by James P O'Shaughnessy and *Reminiscences Of A Stock Operator* by Edwin Lefevre. The former was published in the late 1990s and examines how 15 different investment strategies fared in the 45 years up to its publication. One section examines whether a firm's share price is set to do well if the company's directors are buying its stock. The same factor, of course, plays an important role in Nimmo's own stock selection matrix. Lefevre's book is much older, dating from the 1920s, but is viewed as something of an investment classic. 'Lefevre called himself a stock plunger, which at the time was a colloquial term for an equity investor,' Nimmo says. 'Now, he was a bit of a dealer, but the book is full of homilies about what to do and what to avoid. It has lots of pithy quotes, like "the trend is your friend". Lefevre made lots of money, although he lost a lot, too, because he didn't follow his own advice.' Keen-eyed readers will have noted that 'the trend is your friend' principle makes an appearance in Nimmo's own stock selection matrix, which looks for companies whose share prices display a positive, upward trend.

INVESTMENT STYLE

Nimmo's fund management approach is rigorous and systematic. It comprises a three-stage investment process that sets out his objectives, screens the stockmarket for investment opportunities then researches thoroughly the companies thrown up as opportunities.

A number of stocks have found a long-term home in Standard Life UK Smaller Companies. Some have been in the fund ever since its launch in 1997. There are two that Nimmo feels exemplify his stock selection process particularly well. The first is UK housebuilder McCarthy & Stone, a specialist in retirement housing. The housebuilder's share price was about 120p when it was bought in 1997 but has since risen past 530p. The company operates in a growth industry, benefits from barriers to entry and has a high market share, three of the key attributes Nimmo looks for in a stock that passes the matrix screening process. 'Demographic trends favour the retirement housing industry, since the number of older people in the UK is rising, so it's a growth area,' he says. 'Building a development of flats also consumes a lot of money. But retirement housebuilders have to construct an entire development before selling it – they can't construct it in plots like conventional housebuilders. So McCarthy & Stone has a bit of a barrier to entry there. The firm also has a very high market share, some 67% of the housing retirement market. So it is a dominant player.'

The second firm Nimmo highlights is UK food retailer Greggs, a firm he feels has a strong company culture. 'Greggs is basically in the lunching business, providing food for the mass market,' he says. 'It focuses on good quality and on good price, but it isn't the sort of

NIMMO'S PERFORMANCE OVER 5 YEARS (31/08/98 - 31/08/03)

||| Harry Nimmo's personal performance in UK Smaller Companies sector
■ Average fund manager performance in UK Smaller Companies sector
■ FTSE SmallCap (Excluding Investment Trusts)

Total Returns (%) / Month End

* For further information see p192   Source: Citywire

place that sells fancy avocado and pine nut sandwiches. It's in a growing market – growing by something like 8-10% per year – and tends to beat analysts' expectations for how much it is likely to earn each year. Its earnings per share have grown 12% per year for the last 30 years, so its shares do well over time. But one of the most distinctive things about it is that it has a very strong company culture – its staff turnover is low and many employees own shares in the company.'

Nimmo illustrates the point about Greggs' strong company culture by describing conversations he has had with the firm's managing director, Mike Darrington, about conducting a 'stock split'. Such an action would split one Greggs share into a number of shares. The rationale for the split is that there are relatively few Greggs shares in issue. This is reflected by the fact that they were worth 135p when the firm floated on the stockmarket in 1984, but are now trading at about £30. A stock split would increase the number of Greggs shares in issue and so lower the price of each share, making it easier to buy and sell them. Such an increase in 'marketability' could draw more investors to the stock, boosting its price. A stock split would make no difference to Greggs employees with shares in the company. Instead of owning a few high-priced shares, they would own more numerous lower-priced shares with the same overall value. But Darrington is reluctant to authorise a stock split, as Nimmo explains: 'I keep on saying that there has to be a stock split since the share price is over £30. But Mike says to me, "Harry, I prefer the message given by retaining the same basis with the 1984 float price. It helps keep the score. In any case, my employees, some of who are not well versed in the ways of the stockmarket, may find it confusing."'

Investors can draw many lessons from Nimmo's approach to fund management. Perhaps the most important is that you should pick an investment strategy and stick to it. Picking stocks systematically relative to agreed objectives and selection criteria is more likely to yield success than haphazardly buying shares that look good for disparate reasons. Equally important is Nimmo's restrained objective, which is to achieve top quartile performance. The insight here is that a greedy investor who goes for big gains will probably end up with a risky portfolio and be at greater risk of losing his shirt. Lastly, like most successful investors, Nimmo spends a lot of time researching and keeping abreast of his investments. It is a time-consuming and painstaking approach to fund management, but then no-one said making money from the stockmarket was easy.

Part 2

The Small-cap
Effect

Astake in a smaller company fund is thought to be an important element of a well-diversified investment portfolio. Investors who dabble directly in the stockmarket also commonly invest some of their money into smaller company shares. In the UK about 8-10% of the money invested in mainstream UK equity funds is committed to small-cap funds. Across the Atlantic 16.5% of the $3 trillion invested in equities through mutual funds can be found in the Aggressive Growth sector, which features many small-cap portfolios. Smaller company stocks are traditionally viewed as riskier than large-cap shares. However, over the long term, investors hope to be adequately rewarded for the extra risk they take. This trade-off between risk and reward is why experts recommend that investors put only a minority of their investment portfolios into small-caps. If things go wrong, investors will feel the pain but will not be wiped out. However, good performance from small-cap shares or funds could substantially boost an investment portfolio's overall return.

For the modern investor small-cap stocks first came to prominence between the mid-1970s and 1988, a period which Nimmo describes as a golden age for small-cap investing. 'From 1975 to 1988, smaller companies as a group put in spectacular and consistent performance,' he says. 'Over that period, the sector was seen as a one-way bet, returning over 100% more than large company stocks'. The performance disparity between small- and large-cap stocks was so great that stockmarket aficionados coined a new piece of jargon, the 'smaller company effect', to describe it. The disparity also encouraged academics in the UK to create a new stockmarket index for small-caps, the Hoare Govett Smaller Companies index. The index was unveiled in 1987 by its creators Professors Elroy Dimson and Paul Marsh of the London Business School, who researched the history of small-cap stocks thoroughly enough to provide index values all the way back to 1955. Extensive number-crunching based on the index suggested that small stocks had consistently performed better than large stocks between 1955 and 1988. Figures like these encouraged more people to believe in the smaller company effect. Investment firms capitalised on the trend by launching a number of new funds dedicated to the sector.

There was much debate about why the smaller company effect existed, but no conclusive answers. Some made the simple point that small companies were young and able to grow quickly, delivering good gains to shareholders along the way. In contrast, established blue-chip firms generally find it harder to post high growth levels. Others argued that far fewer people analysed small companies compared with large-caps. This left many investment opportunities in the small-cap sector unrecognised, they contended, storing up big gains for the few who did their homework and backed small-cap stocks. Yet, ironically, just as this debate was in flow, and just as investors jumped on the smaller company bandwagon, the good run enjoyed by small-caps came to an end. 'August 1988 was the peak and marked the start of a long bear market in small-cap stocks relative to large-cap stocks,' Nimmo explains. 'It was a bear market that lasted just over 10 years until December 1998.'

A complex story lies behind small-cap stocks' reversal of fortune. Some of the blame in the UK lies with the painful economic recession that blighted the country in the early 1990s. The downturn hit small companies particularly badly. However, more general trends affecting the fund management industry on both sides of the Atlantic were also at play. They had the effect of concentrating ever greater sums of money in the largest companies, leaving smaller company stocks in the shade. All this happened because the amount of money committed to the stockmarket by pension funds, firms and private investors grew massively in the 1990s. Fund managers faced the problem of how to manage such large sums of money and decided to invest in large firms. They were reassured by the fact that big firms were very well researched and offered shares that could be traded in large quantities quite easily. Of course, as more money was committed to large-cap shares, their price rose, attracting yet more investors. Eventually, investing in large-caps came to be seen as a sure-fire way to make a healthy return. Small-caps, in contrast, suffered a slump in performance and popularity.

The modern stockmarket reflects the rise and dominance of large-cap stocks. In the UK the FTSE SmallCap index contains 340 firms ranging in market capitalisation from a lowly £11 million up to £260 million. There are 693 stocks in the UK FTSE All Share index, so small firms account for nearly half of these in number. However, the combined market capitalisation of small-cap stocks is worth just 2% of the FTSE All Share's capitalisation, which is equal to about £1.2 trillion. In contrast, the biggest 100 companies in the FTSE 100 index account for 80% of the FTSE All Share's capitalisation. Similarly, large-caps dominate small-caps in the US. The S&P 500 index of America's largest 500 firms has a market capitalisation in excess of $9 trillion, while the S&P SmallCap 600 has a market capitalisation of just $400 billion.

The dominance of large firms combined with small firms' fall from grace has led some to question whether the smaller company effect exists at all. One way to make a stab at answering the question is to look at the very long-term statistics compiled by Dimson and Marsh in conjunction with investment bank ABN Amro. These figures are quite striking. They show that £1000 invested into small-cap stocks in 1955 would have been worth about £1.1 million by the end of 2002. In contrast, a £1000 investment into the UK stockmarket as a whole would have grown to about £370,000. So small-caps beat the overall stockmarket by a factor of three over the 48-year period. Of course, the key question is whether the future will resemble the past, with small firms outdoing large ones over the very long term. No-one really knows the answer, which only time will tell. Nimmo's best guess is that small-caps are set to do well for a few years, having spent the 1990s in the doldrums. Investors, for their part, are likely to carry on committing a slice of their investment portfolios to small stocks in the hope that the smaller company effect is alive and kicking.

David Ross
Crunching the Numbers

by Richard Lander

*L*ike fly-fishing or origami, quantitative investing is often derided
by those who don't understand it. Many dismiss it as the
abdication of investor responsibility to a computer. How, they
ask, can a box of bits, bytes and silicon have that all-important
'instinct' that many investors deem vital to successful fund management? Why not just give monkeys darts to throw at the stock price
pages? The answer, of course, is that quantitative investing involves
enormous amounts of human input – perhaps more than traditional
investing. And the key to success is just the same – the greater the
talent behind the methodology, the better the results that will emerge.

Testing for Success

Y ou don't have to be a rocket scientist to be a quantitative investor; sometimes it helps to have studied something a little more obscure. Take David Ross, who heads up the quantitative equities team at Old Mutual Asset Managers (OMAM). Nothing so mainstream as rocket science for Ross – he studied quantum physics, a subject 'even more theoretical than rocket science'.

Happily for those worried about the lack of rocket scientists at OMAM, one member of Ross' team, John O'Brien, did spend some time working on projects for the European Space Agency. Ross says 'a disproportionate number of people following a quantitative approach to investment do have a physics background.' And while many might say that the relationship between quantum physics and stockmarket investment is an obscure one at best, he can see a useful parallel. 'They're both very mathematical – both use maths to understand, describe and explain real-world phenomena.'

What you really do need for quantitative investing – far more than an understanding of the way a rocket gets into orbit – is patience. It's a very research-driven process – in a way, far more so than that used by investors who spend days poring over analyst reports. Processes are theorised, developed, tested, back-tested, applied and refined in an almost endless iterative process.

Quantitative investing is a long and winding road, at the end of which is no magic formula for finding the perfect stock. No quantitative investor has ever dropped everything, run into the nearest bar and shouted, 'We've found the secret of life!'. That's strictly for scientists. A quant man or woman is more likely to raise an eyebrow and smile quietly before checking things over and re-evaluating every assumption.

Despite his scientific background, Ross was by no means predestined to be a quantitative fund manager. He spent 10 years as a traditional runner of money – first with Nomura and then, from 1995, with OMAM – before developing an interest in the numerical side as he saw its growing potential. The opportunity to build a serious active quantitative business came in 1998 when OMAM gave him *carte blanche* to start a greenfield operation. It took a full 18 months to build up the investment approach before the first long-only funds were launched at the beginning of 2000 in both retail and institutional flavours. Market-neutral hedge funds, which Ross thinks are a natural fit for quant investing, followed at the end of 2001. After three years Ross' six regional quantitative funds can boast superior performances against benchmarks over one, two and three years, backed by good returns for his hedge and institutional funds.

Ross considers his style of investing to be pretty close to one extreme of the quantitative approach. At one end are what he calls the 'Stat Arbs' – the purest of pure number-crunchers who employ a very large and powerful computer to help develop trading rules before they go out and trade. At the other end are quants like Ross. 'People like us don't crunch a single number until we have developed a theory that our approach might work,' he explains. 'We formulate it and test it and only then do we think about implementing it. Our aim is to come up with decisions that are logical and explicable and not just based on the fact that "the numbers say it has to work".'

Ross thinks that the number-crunching approach adopted by some of the 'extreme' rocket scientists in the quant business has two major failings. 'The first concerns the fallibility of data-mining. Throwing a Cray supercomputer at the problem won't solve things. Any set of data will throw up numbers that you could back-test to make you money. It's a bit like getting monkeys to type Shakespeare – the monkeys might get to do it eventually but they won't be able to tell you how or why.' Follow this logic, says Ross, and you might as well base your selections on companies with between seven and nine letters in their name or on those whose chairmen have red hair.

The second problem with the 'numbers and nothing else' school is coping with your choice of investment criteria if they don't work on a live market. 'In these sorts of circumstances you have no framework to understand why it worked in the past and why it fails to work now. You face a host of questions that you are in no position to answer, such as "Has anything changed? Is it going wrong because of one month's 'noise' in the market, or is it something more permanent? Do I need to change my approach?"'

The major building block for Ross' approach to investment is a relative return model that provides a forecast return for more than 3000 stocks traded around the world. It comprises five weighted factors that are crunched for each stock:

* Value (based on a discounted cashflow valuation).
* Earnings revision (a relatively low weighting – and almost non-existent for US stocks now that the whole market studies this factor).
* Stock momentum.
* Sector momentum.
* Management hubris. This is based on two objective events centred around changes in a company's capital structure. 'First of all, insiders will issue equity when a company's stock is overvalued and buy it back when it is undervalued for obvious reasons. I think the market tends to underestimate this,' says Ross. 'Secondly, and related to this, acquisitions lead to equity issuance in many cases, and when this happens a company tends to underperform.'

So, for any given stock the exposure for each factor is multiplied

---

DAVID ROSS: THE MAN

David Ross was born in 1964 and is married with one daughter. When not crunching numbers he likes to study architecture. He has an MA in Theoretical Physics from Cambridge University. He is also an affiliate of the Society of Investment Professionals and a corporate member of the Institute for Quantitative Investment Research.

by the weight, and the end result is a forecast percentage return. The table below shows Ross' assessment of BT in mid-2003. Unusually, each factor has a positive rating, making BT a very favourable stock for Ross' buy list.

Before any stock gets onto the buy list, however, other hurdles have to be jumped. Risk is one of them, and Ross thinks his approach is different from other investors in that he gives equal importance to risk. 'A lot of people put a lot of effort into return and regard risk as a constraint. We think it should be integral to the process, and so put a lot of effort into it with the aim of maximising return per unit of risk.'

Ross tends to use bespoke packages for measuring risk, aiming to restrain tracking error for his long-only funds and absolute volatility for his hedge funds. Once the risk and return numbers have been run, and after a final sanity check, a stock will make it to the trade list. At this point, the cost advantages of quantitative trading come into play, with the portfolios updated, usually every month with a programme trade (this is where shares are traded 'wholesale', thereby minimising costs). 'It is cheaper and more efficient than a normal agency trade. And there is no reason why we should bother to use a broker because we don't use their sell-side research.'

If all this sounds a bit clinical, Ross goes to some pains to emphasise that there is an enormous amount of human intervention behind his investment process. The mathematics and the modelling are not

Old Mutual Asset Managers Forecast Return for BT Group			Source: OMAM
Return Factors	Weight of Factor	BT Factor Exposure	BT Forecast Contributions
Value Factors	4.25	0.94	3.97%
Earnings Revisions	3.45	0.06	0.21%
Stock Momentum	4.40	0.16	0.70%
Management Hubris	3.49	1.17	4.10%
Sector Momentum	2.31	2.73	6.30%
Forecast return			15.28%

the dominant features of his working day, and nor are they the sole reason why he thinks his methodology works better than others. Indeed, in among the number-crunching is a surprising amount of philosophy. 'Investing in the way we do is not merely about having a morbid interest in numbers,' he says. 'Rather, I would say that our quantitative approach is only a tool kit for serious objective analysis. We can't outperform the market simply because we think that we are so clever. But we can outperform with the right approach.'

This is where the philosophical side of Ross' strategy comes in, allowing him to use his mathematical underpinnings to achieve superior performance. 'Investors are human beings who diverge from the norms, and they do so by exhibiting behavioural problems. We are then able to exploit these anomalies without falling into the same traps that they do.'

One example of these enlightening behavioural traits is the unbalanced way in which investors sell stocks that they have made or lost money in. 'There is very clear evidence that investors have a tendency to sell shares that have made a profit, but hold on to ones that are running at a loss.' Ross describes this as the 'disposition effect' which is, at heart, a reflection of the pride that human beings show – both inside and outside investment circles – and their unwillingness to admit they have made a mistake.

'If you believe that momentum strategies tend to work, you might ask, "So what?" But, looking at it this way, you can see shares falling as other people are selling winners, and this gives us a welcome opportunity to buy a share we are keen on at somewhat less than the optimum price.'

An original thinker, Ross is keen to highlight how different his approach is, not just from more conventional methods of stock-picking but also from other quantitative followers in the market. One major difference is in the way he treats markets – he sees them as part of one global universe, rather than as separate entities obeying their own behavioural rules. 'We definitely have a global approach – we want something that will work across the world. If, for example, we find that a return factor works in the London market but not in the

US, then it doesn't engender much confidence that it will continue to work in the UK,' he explains.

The consequences of this can be quite costly in terms of intellectual grey matter expended to reach a working formula. 'A lot of quant shops have different desks for each market. But we stick to one global desk. The downside is that we tend to throw away a lot of ideas that work well in one market because they don't work elsewhere.'

Ross likes to compare and contrast his way of investing, and stress-tests its advantages against more fundamental approaches. One such perceived advantage is his success in selecting stocks to short in his hedge funds. 'People find it extremely difficult to move from running long-only portfolios to running hedge funds,' he says. 'There are lots of different issues here but one in particular is the ability to pick short candidates. It is great being a really good stock-picker on the positive side, but much, much harder on the negative side.'

Intuitively that sounds correct. Fundamental fund managers are bombarded with information, especially in the form of stockbroking research which, for many reasons, stresses a particular stock's positive qualities rather than its flaws. 'By contrast, our research models tend to throw up about 50% negative candidates that you can easily exploit in a hedge fund,' he says.

It is always intriguing to ask quantitative or technically-oriented analysts and fund managers about how they would react if the evidence of the real world was opposite to what their computers were telling them. An extreme example of this would be, say, if a chartist

---

CAREER PROFILE

- 1987-1990: UK equity manager at Royal London.
- 1990-1995: Nomura Capital Management.
- 1995-present: Old Mutual Asset Managers, where his quantitative equities team manages a wide range of funds including Old Mutual European Equity, Old Mutual North American Equity and Old Mutual Global Equity funds. He is also responsible for the Old Mutual Global Equity Market Neutral Fund Limited and the Old Mutual Gem Plus Fund Limited hedge funds, along with millions of pounds in other mandates.

got a very strong buy signal from his graphs for a particular company on the same day that its chief executive was arrested for burning all the factories to the ground.

Ross' decision over whether to buy a particular company for whom his model is hugely positive is unlikely to be influenced by traditional managers' views on individual stocks. 'If, say, my colleague Ashton Bradbury tells me that a company's management are making up the numbers from thin air then, yes, I would be concerned,' Ross concedes. 'But, in general, we agree to differ.'

In contrast to Bradbury's more holistic approach to investing, Ross focuses on the numbers. 'I see stocks as probability plays on which you can play the odds. My other response might be to tell him that he was wrong!' In fact, as Ross points out, the two men do very different jobs. 'Ashton holds a more concentrated portfolio and drills down in huge detail. We have a far shallower but much wider set of positions. In essence, we're playing the odds across many stocks.'

But Ross has no intention of putting his life savings on red and waiting for the wheel to spin in his favour – not even if the forecast return on a particular stock indicates that it is a screaming buy. 'Yes, the numbers can shout "Fill your boots" over a stock, but you have to understand the limits of numbers – a big score for a particular stock might contain a lot of statistical noise.' This is one reason why the trading list is always inspected for common sense. Another reason, in the case of the hedge fund, is to check whether a particular stock can be borrowed for shorting purposes at a reasonable price.

In fact, Ross' portfolios are very conservative by any measure. They

---

INVESTMENT STYLE

The investment approach used by the quantitative equities team seeks to exploit market inefficiencies by employing rigorous quantitative research, based on investment insights and objective evidence. The approach focuses equally on risk and return, and aims to generate a highly diversified portfolio with favourable risk return characteristics. It is used to run equity funds investing in the UK, US, Continental Europe and Japan, as well as on a global scale.

are all on the large side – from 80 companies for the UK fund to 300 for the global fund, and an eye-popping 800 for the hedge fund.

On top of that 'we are never more than 1% overweight in a stock, no matter how much we like it.' Ross reckons it is just not worth going any further out on a limb and has the numbers to prove his point. 'We simulated a back-test over the 1980s and 1990s that showed that a 1% overweight rule is superior to a 2% one. So we simply wouldn't get enough reward for the extra risk.'

The hedge funds, meanwhile, are market neutral. In other words, long and short exposures are equally matched with a zero net exposure. Again, Ross reckons the temptation to take an active bet one way or another would not reap any reward. 'In theory, yes. If a manager has a strong skill at calling the overall market direction then fine, go net one way or another. But sadly the reality is that there is very limited evidence that managers have that skill. And at least being market neutral has the virtue of allowing investors in the hedge fund to have assets truly uncorrelated with their other investments.'

Spend an hour with David Ross and the logic of the quantitative investment process starts to come home. It is a difficult process to understand because it is far removed from the way most managers invest, not just for private investors and interested amateurs, but for some City professionals as well.

'The message of how we manage funds is a problem both for private client intermediaries and the actuaries who advise institutions on who should manage their money,' says Ross. 'They can see the merits of what we do – and they very much appreciate our equal emphasis on risk – but they find it difficult to communicate that message to the end-users who they advise.'

The answer to the problem is obvious – perform well, as Ross' funds are doing, and investors will believe the message. In the end, as Ross says, the numbers he uses in the way he invests are neither here nor there – it is what you do with them that counts.

The Numbers Game

Active quantitative equity management is to investment what the hamburger is to the culinary arts – invented in the US, it is getting bigger every year and is increasingly known wherever you go in the world.

Its progress has followed the development of computers and communications over the years. Four decades ago you needed a roomful of computers to run the very first crude quantitative models. These were effectively stock screens, overlaying several numerical criteria about a company – perhaps its dividend, growth rate, P/E ratio and capitalisation – to filter a large stock universe into a manageable portfolio. The process was laborious, could take hours to yield results and had to be run by experts.

Today, desktop computers are able to process quantitative information in ever increasing amounts, updating the results in real time. The number of techniques used in the quant process has also increased. Many of them are based on developments from scientific disciplines, such as statistics, physics and biology, and include fractal theory, fuzzy logic and genetic algorithms. And on the output side, the number of outlets where quant investing can be used has grown enormously, ranging from complex arbitrage instruments to futures, options and hedge funds.

None of these trends is likely to be reversed, and the sums of money managed by quant techniques – already well into trillions of dollars, will grow exponentially. Moore's law, which predicts that computing power doubles every three years, remains firmly in place. On top of that, the potential to harness the combined processing power of massive networks of computers – so called grid computing – has hardly been tapped.

The reasons why quant investing found its feet in the US are not hard to understand. Apart from having more software engineers and financial academics than anywhere else in the world, the US' reputation as the land of plenty was another spur. Competitive pressures, market liquidity, and volume of information are all traditionally much bigger in the US than elsewhere. Plus, Americans have a penchant for measuring and testing things that goes beyond anything seen anywhere else in the world. From baseball performance to factory productivity, the American adage is 'if you can't measure it, don't do it'.

Talk to proponents of active quant equity investing and they will come up with a host of other reasons why their approach is the best one to follow. In a paper published in 2002 Acadian Asset Management, a Boston-based quantitative investment house, which is also part of the Old Mutual empire, enumerated the following distinct advantages.

Breadth
Put simply, the more stocks you follow in your investment appraisal, the better your results. Of course, in the fundamental world a great fund manager who covers 20 stocks will get better results than a seriously bad one who covers 100. But with two managers of equal skill, the one covering more stocks should do better.

Nobody can accuse quant systems of lack of breadth. Whereas a fundamental manager could probably get to know, at the very outside, 1000 companies, even then he or she would see each company only once a year, and that's assuming they meet four companies a day and have no holidays. Because computers don't take holidays or slope off early on Fridays, coverage of universes of 20,000 stocks are feasible, with each company crunched using a myriad of valuation fundamentals including every earnings forecast from every analyst. As Acadian puts it: 'What we have built over a number of years is an "automated security analyst" making continuously updated alpha forecasts on thousands of global equities every day.'

A refinement of this point is that conventional managers and analysts generally have a gradation of knowledge about companies – some they know very well, others less well, and others only a little. A quant process by contrast knows each company to the same degree, a key advantage, according to Acadian, because it 'means our forecasts are truly comparable across stocks and we have no bias towards buying a stock that we simply happen to know more about.'

Objectivity

Nobody ever fooled a computer into buying a stock after taking it for a good dinner and a night on the town. Of course, top-rated analysts and fund managers will claim they are never influenced by how they are treated by a company. But there is no denying that human emotions – the same ones that make top managers good in the first place – can sometimes be counter-productive. Most managers at some time have fallen in love with a stock. Like true love this can make them oblivious to the faults of their loved one and, in a stock's case, they may fail to sell it when the time is right.

Quant followers argue that their approach does away with the blurring mists that emotions can bring. In particular, it can throw up a contradictory investment process, so that when the herd is screaming for a particular stock or sector, a quant's computer process is saying it is time to get out and go for the overlooked stocks.

Behavioural errors

Remember the 'new paradigm' of 2000 when Internet stocks went through the roof, reaching infinite P/E multiples because they had no earnings? Several fund managers who should have known better claimed we had entered a new era of commerce where the old rules of investing didn't count. Likening themselves to old dogs, quants claimed that their computers prevented them from falling for new tricks like this one. The Internet boom was, on a huge scale, a display of collective behavioural errors that made investors lose the plot completely. Some of these errors cited by Acadian include:

* Loss aversion (investors become risk-averse when faced with a loss).
* Overconfidence (investors think they have more skill than they actually do).
* Extrapolation (investors think current trends are likely to continue).
* Anchoring (investors pay excessive attention to old information and under-react to new information).

Again, quants argue that their investment process avoids all these behavioural errors. If a stock is too expensive on the basis of the quantitative investment process, then it is time for it to be sold. The fact that perhaps it is being sold at a huge loss – an emotionally difficult process for fundamental managers and the reason they often hold on to a stock while it goes further south – is neither here nor there. If the process says it has to be sold, it goes.

Costs

OMAM's quantitative funds buy and sell stocks through programme trades, avoiding the cost of agency commissions. In general, quant managers place a strong emphasis on keeping trading costs down and try to fully integrate them into the portfolio decision-making instead of treating them as a burden on performance they can do little about.

So if quant investing is so good, why doesn't everybody do it? Aside from the fact that few managers feel equipped to do it, there are downsides to the approach that quants themselves recognise and do their best to minimise. Two in particular stand out. The first is that quant processes rely on historical evidence. In other words, stock A should be bought because it has always risen by at least 20% when events B and C have happened together. But markets change, and these relationships change, so the outcome could be very different this time.

New industries also present a problem. The quant managers whose processes told them not to buy the flakiest Internet companies were proved right in the end – but they had to suffer a long period of underperformance relative to the market and to those managers who jumped on the bandwagon.

Ask any quant manager what is the hardest part about selling his process to an adviser or consultant and he or she will tell you 'they're all convinced that the computers have taken over'. No-one really likes the idea of a grey box running their clients' precious money, especially when they often find their own computers to be difficult and unreliable.

The message that needs to get across is that no matter how big and powerful the box, it needs a powerful set of brains behind it to come up with some decent investment decisions. As Brad Lawson of the huge Russell investment group wrote in a research article, *Evaluating Quantitative Managers*, even the most computerised portfolio construction model has to have human input to get it going: 'Subjectivity and insight are used to create the models, which contain the decision rules for selecting stocks.'

Lawson's same piece laid down three ground rules for finding good quantitative managers:

* 'Quantitative models are designed, built and generated by investment professionals. Therefore, just as in the evaluation of fundamental managers, experience, professional capability and capacity are integral to assessing the potential success of the process.'

* 'It is important to distinguish and favour managers who view models as a means to an end... over managers caught up solely in the intricacies of model-building for its own sake.'

* 'The process must be easily interpreted by humans and flexible enough to allow revision – perhaps, for instance, discarding factors that have not enhanced outcomes.'

The bottom line is simple – computers have not taken over just yet.

Anthony Nutt
Thriving on Income Support

by Sunil Jagtiani

*M*ost investors are first attracted to the stockmarket by the capital gains they think they can make, rather than by the dividends paid to shareholders by firms. The chance for big profits from rising share prices seems to them to dwarf dividend payments. Dividends are typically worth a very small percentage of a firm's share price, a figure often in low single digits, while many firms pay no dividends at all. However, taking such an approach to the stockmarket is a mistake. Buying shares for the dividends they pay, the art of equity income investing, can be a successful way to make money from stocks. Moreover, dividends are crucial to the long-term stockmarket returns investors can expect to enjoy. This chapter looks at the investment techniques of Anthony Nutt, a successful UK equity income investor, and goes on to show how important equity dividends are to all investors.

Part 1

The Income
Nutt

A nthony Nutt is one of the UK's best-known equity income fund managers. His prominence rests on the fact that he successfully runs one of the UK's largest and most popular equity income funds, the £1.5 billion Jupiter Income unit trust. Nutt has worked at Jupiter Unit Trust Managers since late 1995, and in January 1996 launched the Jupiter High Income fund, a UK equity and bond unit trust now £300 million strong. He has won plaudits for his performance record at the helm of both funds. A £1000 investment in the High Income fund was worth £1488 by mid-2003, assuming the income it generated was reinvested into the stockmarket. In contrast, 27 competing equity and bond funds turned £1000 into, on average, £1105. If you put the performance of these 27 funds into a league table, Jupiter High Income beats them all. Nutt's record as manager of the giant Jupiter Income fund, which began in May 2000, is relatively short and covers one of the worst periods in modern stockmarket history. An initial £1000 investment in the fund, with dividend income reinvested, had fallen to £997 by mid-2003. However, rival equity income funds fared even worse, turning the same investment into, on average, £851. The UK stockmarket over the same period fell by 28.16%, which is equivalent to a £282 slide in a £1000 investment.

Given these figures, there seems little doubt that Nutt chose the right profession – eventually. For his career could have taken a very different turn. Born in 1953, Nutt skipped university to join the

British civil service where he ended up working in the controversial world of arm sales at the Ministry of Defence. Some of the Ministry's employees, he notes, opt to work anywhere but the arms sales division over ethical concerns. 'A few of the people we used to look after ended up being assassinated,' he adds. This is one occupational hazard that even the worst fund manager need not worry about. Then, in the mid-1970s, Nutt left the civil service to work in stockbroking and fund management, where he has been ever since.

Thanks to the years he spent at the helm of other giant funds early in his career, Nutt is certainly well qualified to run a fund as large as Jupiter Income. His major career break came in the 1980s when UK banking group Lloyds TSB asked him to run its biggest fund, which at the time had assets of about £1.6 billion. After three years he left to run an even bigger £2 billion fund at blue-blooded UK banking group Flemings. By this stage his reputation as a fund manager was growing. The move to Jupiter took him to a company whose success was built on the work of talented fund managers prepared to back their convictions. The company's culture differs from that of many other investment firms, which give their managers less freedom to shape their funds as they want to.

When Nutt joined Jupiter it was run by John Duffield, a high-profile and occasionally controversial figure. Duffield, a hard taskmaster, had established the firm in 1985. It was soon one of the UK's leading investment houses. In 1995 German firm Commerzbank paid about £170 million to buy 75% of Jupiter. It then purchased the rest of the company in 2000 for £500 million. The latter transaction helped to make some Jupiter employees multi-millionaires, while Duffield himself reportedly made hundreds of millions of pounds. However, it also heralded a watershed for the firm because Duffield

---

ANTHONY NUTT: THE MAN

Anthony Nutt was born in 1953 and is married with four children. He obtained his degree in Philosophy and Economics through the Open University. He keeps fit by cycling.

left later that year in a move anticipated by few onlookers. The split was acrimonious, highly publicised and involved a legal dispute that was eventually settled out of court. It also led to speculation about whether Nutt would leave Jupiter, too, even though he had just taken on the stewardship of Jupiter Income.

Nutt was already under pressure to ensure the fund maintained the excellent performance record established by his predecessor, William Littlewood, who had retired through exhaustion aged just 34. Jupiter Income was the firm's flagship product, the most potent symbol of its success and the second largest equity income fund in the country. Littlewood had practised an idiosyncratic stock-picking style and was the archetype of the star fund manager, which made both investors and commentators wonder how the fund would fare after his departure. Some of these concerns spilled onto the financial sections of national newspapers as fund experts pulled six-figure investments out of Jupiter Income. Ratings agency Standard & Poor's provided more fuel for critics when it cut the fund's top-drawer rating for the first time in two years only a month after Nutt took charge. To top it all off, the stockmarket had entered a period of tumbling share prices that would pose a severe test for even the best investors. Nutt, who had been given only one day's warning that he was to succeed Littlewood, had a heavy responsibility on his shoulders.

EQUITY INCOME INVESTING

Equity income investors aim to generate an attractive income from stock dividends. The majority hope for a good total return comprising dividend payments and capital gains. Income investors tend to select stocks with a higher yield than the average for the stockmarket. Higher-yielding stocks are thought to offer less scope for capital growth, so income investors often invest a proportion of their portfolio into lower-yielding stocks to make capital gains, too. It is up to the income investor to balance income and capital growth as he or she sees fit. Some set out to achieve a higher income yield at the expense of capital growth, while others sacrifice a high yield at the altar of capital gains. Overall, income investors are value investors in search of stocks with attractive P/E ratios. Generally, they seek established firms with reliable revenues that can be used to fund rising dividend payments to shareholders.

In the event, Nutt rose to the occasion, and fears over the future of Jupiter Income proved unfounded. 'Don't forget I was taking the fund over from a guy who sat next to me,' he says. 'So I knew everything he was doing and I knew what was in the fund and why it was there.' Nutt's objective as manager of the 100-stock fund is to invest in shares that are able to deliver a growing dividend income over time. 'I can achieve this in one of two ways,' he explains. 'First, I can invest in shares that are growing their dividends at a higher rate than the average for the stockmarket as a whole. The dividend yield on such shares is less important to me than the fact that the dividends are growing. Second, I can invest in shares with a low yield, but which have the potential to deliver capital gains. I can then reinvest some of those gains in other shares to generate income. In fact, the latter is much more attractive to me than just investing in an equity with a much higher-than-average yield and whose share price stays static. Income investing isn't just about investing in very high-yield shares.'

With the objective set, Nutt then deploys a management style that combines the search for income growth with a hunt for competitively priced shares. 'I just don't think everybody can deploy a bargain-hunting approach,' he says. 'For example, we work in Knightsbridge, a well-heeled area of London, and if you go around the corner you will see people buying very expensive fashion labels. Now, they're never going to make good fund managers. That sort of approach, paying full price for an asset, whether it's a stock, a fashion label or a car, is not attractive to me.' To implement his overall strategy successfully Nutt analyses the economy, its industrial sectors and individual compa-nies. Economic analysis helps to illuminate the profitable investment opportunities created by trends in gross domestic product, inflation and interest rates, to name but a few variables. Nutt will then go on to look at sectors to see whether developments within them have opened or closed investment possibilities. Last but by no means least comes company analysis. The two key elements here are meeting management teams and a close scrutiny of company accounts.

A good practical example of the way economic analysis can throw up concrete investment opportunities is provided by War Loan (debt issued by the British Government between 1914 and 1917 to pay for its involvement in World War One). Jupiter decided to put War Loan into its equity funds in the 1990s. The move left onlookers perplexed since War Loan was generally regarded as, at best, a boring investment or, at worst, a disastrous one. War Loan was issued with an initial value of £100 and since 1932 has paid annual interest of 3.5% based on that initial price, equivalent to £3.50. The capital value of the stock fluctuates according to supply and demand. The value of the stock tumbled in the decades after it was first issued as inflation and interest rates rose. At one stage, in the mid-1970s, War Loan was changing hands at just 17p. However, in the 1990s Jupiter's managers felt inflation and interest rates were going to fall faster than consensus expectations suggested. In fact, interest rates fell from nearly 15% in 1990 to less than 6% in 2000. War Loan was trading at about £40 when Jupiter's managers bought it, so its annual £3.50 interest payment represented a yield of nearly 9%, an attractive figure in a climate of falling interest rates. Sure enough, War Loan drew investors' attention and its price hit nearly £80 by the time Jupiter's managers sold the stock. It turned out to be an investment that delivered a good income and, because of that, good capital growth.

Unlike managers in other companies, Nutt can exercise a degree of

---

⟡ CAREER PROFILE

- 1972-1976: Ministry of Defence.
- 1976-1983: Stockbroker at Foster & Braithwaite.
- 1983-1986: Investment Manager at UKPI/Friends Provident Investment Management.
- 1986-1989: Unit trust investment manager at TSB Investment Management, responsible for their largest UK unit trust.
- 1989-1995: Director of Robert Fleming Asset Management, where he managed UK mandates for overseas clients, specialist pension funds and investment trusts.
- 1995-1996: Director of River & Mercantile Investment Management, where he worked for John Beckwith.
- 1996-present: Jupiter Asset Management, where he runs the Jupiter High Income and Jupiter Income funds, the funds that made his name and which he invests in himself.

personal choice in his decisions about whether or not to back a particular sector. An investor who examined the fund's profile in 2003
would have seen that it had little or no exposure to the oil, pharmaceutical or telecommunications sectors. The rationale for Nutt's
decision was that he expected the price of oil to weaken following the
war in Iraq in March 2003, while the share prices of pharmaceutical
and telecommunications companies looked expensive. 'In some fund
management companies you just don't have the scope to exercise
your judgement like this,' he says. This is because many investment
firms view managers who have the courage to back their convictions
as too great a risk should they get it wrong. Instead, these firms will
note how much of the UK stockmarket a particular sector accounts for
– in the case of oil and gas the figure is 12.5% – and tell their
managers to invest a similar proportion of their fund into it, allowing
them only limited room for manoeuvre around that figure. 'At some
stage fund managers and investment firms have to decide whether
they want to manage business risk or their funds,' Nutt says.

Nutt judges whether he likes a company by analysing its accounts
thoroughly and by meeting its senior management team, usually the
chief executive and the finance director. A US company, the Centre for
Financial Research and Analysis (CFRA), assists with the analysis of
accounts. The firm goes through the accounts of UK firms with a
fine-toothed comb and reports its findings regularly. The reports highlight issues that often escape analysts at investment banks but could
materially affect the performance of a company's share price. One
example is provided by CFRA's 2003 report on WPP, an international
communications services firm listed on the London Stock Exchange
and on Nasdaq. The document warns that the firm 'may have
provided itself with the opportunity to boost reported profits in 2001,
and possibly in future periods, by utilising aggressive accounting in

---

INVESTMENT STYLE

Nutt is a value investor who searches for stocks that can deliver a
growing income and are competitively priced.

conjunction with its November 2001 acquisition of Tempus'. The CFRA report then goes on to detail its concerns, providing a level of company intelligence that most private investors and many rival fund managers miss out on, preferring to spend their money and time on other things.

Nutt says the key to management meetings is to watch and listen carefully. 'As a fund manager it's very important to listen to the messages,' he says. 'Far too many people in today's stressful world are on transmit only. Some years ago I remember going out to Boeing. I had lunch in the staff canteen with Phil Condit, the chairman and chief executive. Now, the staff there would call him by his first name. I noticed that. I like that approach to management, where the boss can relate to his employees. More generally, if I find managers who are clear about what they are doing and who have integrity, then it's easier to follow them. At my age – I'm 50 – it's a lot easier to see through corporate flannel, because you don't see many new characters. Most people seem to come from one well-known mould or another. But basically I'm looking to come out of a management meeting thinking that I really understand the financial consequences of where a chief executive plans to take his company.'

To this day Nutt recollects a management meeting that triggered one of the biggest stock calls of his career. It happened in 1987, when he was managing the giant £1.6 billion TSB General unit trust. The trust had a major investment in British Plasterboard, known as BPB. 'I remember they had very smart headquarters and use of a gold Rolls Royce for senior members of the management team,' he says. 'They had, effectively, a monopoly in the UK and decided to go into the German market. Well, the Germans said if you come into our market, we'll come into yours, and they did. I found the attitude of BPB's management over this threat alarming. I was a big holder of BPB but I decided to sell my shares. Now, BPB in those days was looking to make £200 million per year, and today, all these years later, it's still only making £190 million. They're big calls – you never forget them.'

Many equity income fund managers adopt a similar approach to that of Nutt. They, too, look for income growth, hunt for reasonably priced stock and analyse economic, industrial and company prospects. So why is it that Nutt is more successful? The answer may lie in two principles underlying his approach to fund management. The first is his belief that investors should stay attuned to the psychology of the stockmarket, in particular the type of investing fashionable with investors at any one time. 'I like to try to understand the mood of the market,' Nutt explains. 'If, as a fund manager, you can identify which valuation criteria the market is adopting from time to time, it will make your job that much easier – half your work is done.'

In the late 1990s, for example, investors were prepared to tolerate higher P/E ratios than used to be the case, which allowed share prices to rise. In contrast, they were less concerned about the low dividend yield offered by shares, even though in the past a low dividend yield was often taken as a sign that share prices were too high. But from 2000 sentiment changed as share prices tumbled. Investors were reluctant to tolerate high P/Es and so attractive dividend yields became an important buy signal for them. An investor on alert for these changes in mood is better placed to exploit them than one who fails to realise that the psychology of the stockmarket shifts over time. The changes during the late 1990s and from 2000 onwards provided Nutt with an opportunity to make capital gains initially, which he then reinvested in shares he felt offered potential for income growth.

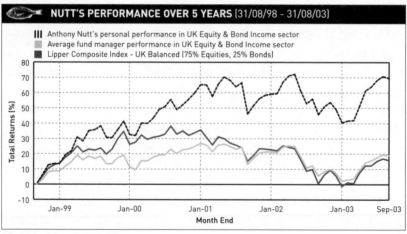

NUTT'S PERFORMANCE OVER 5 YEARS (31/08/98 - 31/08/03)

||| Anthony Nutt's personal performance in UK Equity & Bond Income sector
Average fund manager performance in UK Equity & Bond Income sector
Lipper Composite Index - UK Balanced (75% Equities, 25% Bonds)

Total Returns (%)

Month End

* For further information see p192

Source: Citywire

The second principle underlying his approach to investment is that investors should never gamble on a stock. 'If fund managers are poor it's generally because they're not investing, they're gambling,' Nutt says. 'You see individuals, however they articulate it, that are gambling. Take the world of business. You get people with entrepreneurial flair who can spot a good concept, who take risks and who can market their wares successfully. Then you get the administrators, the boardroom politicians, who tend to be the bean counters. They're the sort of people who run large companies. In fund management you get similar styles. And I think the guy going out on a limb and gambling, rather than being considered, is the one more likely to struggle with his performance. It's all about having confidence in your judgements rather than taking a flier and hoping it comes off.'

A spectacular example of the principle in action is provided by the sad tale of Marconi, a one-time industrial giant whose name is now synonymous with perhaps the most catastrophic collapse in British corporate history. The firm, previously called GEC, was carefully and methodically built up over 33 years by Arnold Weinstock, better known as Lord Weinstock, until he retired in 1996. He left behind a very profitable defence and electrical conglomerate with a market capitalisation of £11 billion and £3 billion of cash reserves. Lord Weinstock was succeeded by George Simpson, another Lord. His vision for the firm was radically different. He and finance director John Mayo set about turning a boring conglomerate into a major supplier of equipment essential for telecommunications and the Internet.

So GEC became Marconi, sold off its established subsidiaries and spent billions acquiring telecommunications equipment firms. Demand for Marconi's products soared during 1999, as businesses young and old rushed to upgrade their technology in time for a new millennium they expected would be revolutionised by the Internet. At one point the firm was worth £35 billion as its share price soared past £12. But the frenzy faded, demand dried up and Marconi's profits collapsed. The hype around the Internet dissipated, leaving too many telecommunications equipment suppliers chasing too few orders. Marconi had to sack thousands of employees and was burdened with more than £4 billion of debt, while its billion-pound acquisitions became practically worthless. By August 2002 the firm's share price had collapsed to a paltry 1.7p, giving it a market capitalisation of just £50 million. Marconi survived the disaster, but the damage was irreparable.

'I looked at Marconi quite carefully when it was changing,' Nutt says. 'I went to have lunch with Mayo, and I listened to what he said and to how negative he was about Lucent and Cisco, rival telecommunications equipment suppliers. And I remember thinking to myself, "Well, if you're right about those businesses then the way you've reformed your business makes me very insecure." I'd taken along our technology fund manager with me, and the judgement we had to make was whether Marconi was going to be a significant business in the telecommunications equipment industry in the future. We decided not to invest. We weren't prepared to gamble. We weren't prepared to say, "We think Marconi is going to be a big player in the field of telecommunications equipment because it's got great technology and a strong balance sheet; I wonder if they can pull it off, let's see." There was just no empirical evidence to enable you to make that call. We couldn't see the complete value destruction that happened, but we could see the potential.'

Nutt's investment style, then, is based not just on traditional economic, industrial and company analysis, but also on psychology. Part of the secret of his success is that he tries to understand the way other investors are thinking to exploit the mood of the market. But he also makes sure he approaches his job correctly, by investing systematically rather than gambling. 'Much of the discipline of fund management is about mental approach,' Nutt says. 'It's about understanding risks and management strategy, about keeping your cool when the pendulum swings from extreme to extreme and being able to think further out rather than being obsessed by short-term issues.' And he has a simple but powerful point to make about the importance of dividend income from equities. 'At the end of the day the value of a business is simply the capital that its investors can take out of it during its lifetime,' he says. 'Everything else is pure speculation.'

Part 2

The Importance
of Dividends

I nvesting in equities for dividends rather than just capital growth
has a long tradition in the mutual fund industry. America's very
first mutual fund, the Massachusetts Investors Trust, launched in
1924 by MFS Investment Management, made the provision of a reasonable income one of its major objectives. The $7 billion fund still
exists some 80 years later and continues to strive for dividend income
as a secondary objective behind capital growth. In the years after its
launch equity funds whose primary objective was securing a good
income from dividends emerged on both sides of the Atlantic. In the
UK one of the first such products, launched in the mid-1960s and still
going strong, was the Dividend fund rolled out by investment house
M&G. Equity income investing subsequently ballooned in popularity,
creating an array of funds offering a varied blend of income and
capital growth prospects.

Equity income investing now accounts for a large chunk of fund
management activity in both the US and the UK. According to
research conducted by the Investment Company Institute, US
investors had committed $120 billion to equity income funds by mid-
2003. This figure rises to $1 trillion, one-third of all the money
invested in equities through US mutual funds, when you include
funds with equity income as a significant, if not sole, objective.
According to the UK's Investment Management Association, some
£21 billion had been committed to equity income funds in the UK by

the same date, equivalent to 12% of the total amount invested in equities. Stateside, private investors can choose from more than 300 equity income funds, while their counterparts in the UK have just over 80 options.

So countless numbers of investors on both sides of the Atlantic look forward to regular income payments funded by company dividends. If their investments achieve capital growth, too, they can anticipate a healthy total return. But it is worth stressing that dividends have a wider role than simply providing an income to spend, since they can be reinvested into the stockmarket. Several studies have shown that the process of reinvesting dividends is very important to long-term investment returns. Three London Business School academics, Elroy Dimson, Paul Marsh and Mike Staunton, have produced some of the best-known work on the topic. They showed that $1 dollar invested in the US stockmarket in 1900 would have grown to about $200 a century later if the dividends earned over the period had been spent rather than reinvested into shares. However, if the dividends had been reinvested, the return would have risen to nearly $17,000. There was a similar result for the UK stockmarket: £1 invested in UK equities in 1900 would have risen to about £160 by 2000 if dividends were spent, but nearly £17,000 if the dividends had been reinvested. Clearly, reinvested dividends are crucial to the return you can expect from stockmarket investments.

Given all this you might think that investors could never doubt the importance of dividends, whether for an income or for reinvestment into the stockmarket to boost long-term gains. Yet you only need to take a short trip down memory lane to find a time when they did. In the 1990s many took the view that dividends mattered much less than before. Indeed, many were quite happy to invest in shares paying no dividends at all. Consequently, income investing fell deeply out of favour. By early 2000 investors' disregard for dividends was so entrenched that Philip Coggan, one of the UK's leading financial commentators, was moved to remark in *The Financial Times*: 'The dividend seems to be going the way of the dinosaur and the dodo: investors just don't seem interested in a steady income anymore.'

The cause of the shift in investors' thinking was simple: share prices rose substantially in the 1990s, despite temporary setbacks like the first Gulf War in 1990 and the global financial crisis of 1997, but dividends failed to keep pace. So investors took the view that capital gains were what counted. If they wanted an income from shares, they could simply sell some of their investments to cash in on healthy capital gains. The primacy of capital gains over dividends was most pronounced between 1998 and the first three months of 2000, a period during which the stockmarket rocketed to incredible levels. Investors simply lost interest in dividends, which looked paltry when framed against the massive capital gains offered by soaring share prices.

One way to look at what happened is to examine the stockmarket's dividend yield, which expresses dividend payments as a percentage of share prices. In the early 1980s the dividend yield from the UK's FTSE All Share index fluctuated between about 5% and 7%. By the early 1990s it ranged between 4% and 5.5%, and by 2000 it had fallen to about 2%. The fall reflects the fact that share prices rose substantially over the period at a higher rate than the level of dividend payments. The shift encouraged firms to reassess their dividend policies, just as investors ended up feeling that dividends were less important than they once were. Research by Dimson, Marsh and Staunton reveals that until the late 1980s about 90% of UK firms paid dividends, a figure that fell to about 60% by 2000.

We now know that the years between 1980 and 2000 formed an exceptional period in the history of the stockmarket. It was a time when investors came to think of equity investment as a one-way ticket to substantial capital gains. Such blinkered optimism culminated in a share price bubble, which gave way to a terrible bear market in the early years of the new millennium. Investors deserted equities in their droves, driving prices down even more. For those who continued to invest in shares, drawing dividend income from stock investments became much more important than in the 1990s since it helped to ease the pain of capital losses. Dividends made a comeback and equity income investing enjoyed a renaissance.

The early years of the 21st Century have been marked by a new mood of caution about the capital growth prospects offered by shares. Many investment professionals expect shares to register much lower capital growth than they did in the 1980s and 1990s. Instead of high double-digit percentage growth each year, they predict just single-digit growth. Others wonder if the equity market may simply stay flat over long periods, despite gyrating up and down along the way. A few, the minority, worry that investors will suffer more down the years than the experience of the 1980s and 1990s has prepared them for. But whichever scenario is correct, the renewed popularity of dividends and income investing is here to stay. If capital gains are modest, then dividends, especially if they are reinvested, will help to boost long-term returns. On the other hand, if share prices are broadly flat or fall over long periods, withdrawn dividends will help to make up for disappointing capital performance.

Jonathan Platt
Bonds of Strength

by Richard Lander

*B*uying the investments nobody else wants to consider is commonplace among equity managers, but far less so among bond fund managers. A very different breed of investor, bond managers are usually less involved in the hunt for overlooked underpriced gems. Jonathan Platt is a rare exception – he has delivered superior performance for his funds on a consistent basis by buying a certain type of bond his rivals will not touch. And we're not talking junk bonds here – these are secured instruments backed by significant assets the bondholder can lay claim to if things go wrong.

Part 1

High Security Bond Investing

When a fund manager proudly owns up to being a conservative investor it usually means one of two things. The first is that, yes, he or she *is* conservative to a fault, taking few risks and sticking with the pack, thus turning in some pretty uninspiring returns for those who have entrusted their hard-earned cash to them. The second is that there is more to the manager than meets the eye – he or she has a trick or two up their sleeve that differentiates them from their peers.

Jonathan Platt, head of fixed income at Royal London Asset Management, falls into the second category and has the badges to prove it – a AAA rating from Citywire and leadership in the UK Corporate Bond sector over the past three years. 'My style is a fairly conservative one,' says Platt. 'It recognises that fund managers can be wrong.' Platt has been with Royal London for 18 years, all his working life, in fact, apart from a brief and unhappy dalliance in accountancy after graduation. 'I realise that we are not perfect, but hopefully I will get more decisions right than wrong. That said, the decisions I get wrong in corporate bonds can be very painful.'

It's from these philosophical underpinnings that Platt has constructed a methodology for investing in corporate bonds, the main tenet of which is to run very diversified portfolios with a great deal of emphasis on security.

Platt is also extremely wary about consensus. While this attitude may sound counter-intuitive for a self-confessed conservative investor, it is one that has been key in helping his funds outperform the pack. 'I am extremely sceptical about the consensus because it is usually wrong. I know that sounds arrogant but having invested in the corporate bond market for the best part of 20 years I've found consensus to be wrong very often.' You get the impression that Platt is dismissive of the consensus because of the way people get there – 'generally it is people gathering together because that is where they feel most comfortable.'

Acknowledging that things can go wrong is also an important step to successful investment as far as Platt is concerned. 'Admit that and then you can plan for that eventuality – you know that stocks out there will go wrong, so if you can avoid those companies and their bonds in the long term then you should return very good results.' Indeed, the long-term horizon is important to Platt, who eschews the chase for a quick trading buck. 'One of the quickest ways to lose money is to try to make money in the short term.' Instinctively, he is also against recent trends such as concentrated funds. 'I like to get diversified through the marketplace. There is a lot of emphasis out there on backing your views and heavily concentrating your holdings but it is something that I am just not comfortable with.'

One of the main ways that Platt regards himself as out of step with the huddled masses of bond managers is what he sees as their huge obsession with ratings and their almost obsessive need to only invest in bonds that have been given the once-over by the bond credit-rating firms. In Platt's view, ratings tell only half the story about a particular bond issue. 'Ratings do give you some valuable information about the probability of a bond defaulting,' he admits. 'But what they do not give you is any concept of the value of a bond, the price at which

---

JONATHAN PLATT: THE MAN

Jonathan Platt was born in 1962 and graduated in Politics, Philosophy and Economics from Oxford University. He has been with the same partner for more than 20 years. He enjoys squash, football, cycling and swimming and loves good wine and reading history books.

it is worth buying and what will happen and how much money you might get back if things should go wrong. What that means is that the consensus bond manager ends up just concentrating on probability. So we differentiate ourselves by using non-rated bonds that are secured against assets and should be pretty safe in most economic conditions.'

The typical Platt-administered portfolio, in fact, will have 20-30% of its investments in non-rated bonds. In general, these bonds have no rating either because the issuer decided not to pay the hefty rating fees or because they were originally issued five to 10 years ago, before the dominance of the ratings agencies was almost total.

Herein lies a clue to Platt's attraction to the non-rated sector – it is what he grew up with as an investor. 'It reflects my background in life assurance, when non-rated bonds were the norm and you invested life funds in issues that had some asset security behind them,' he says. A typical non-rated bond still favoured today by Platt will have at least 90% of the money raised on it secured by financial or property assets. One example – and the largest holding in the Royal London unit trust portfolios – is the Foreign & Colonial (F&C) bond, repayable in 2014, which is secured against the assets of the Foreign & Colonial Investment Trust, one of the oldest, largest and most stately investment vehicles around. The security has the first charge against the trust's assets, which means that the bondholders, like a mortgage bank, get their hands on the assets before anybody else should the fund be wound up or get into trouble.

Now, here's the nub of Platt's strategy, which ultimately delivers his superior performance. Bonds like the F&C issue have the safety status of a 'blueish' chip corporate bond with the yield of something riskier – which means more money in a Platt portfolio and fewer issues going wrong. 'The F&C bond would probably have an AA rating if the credit agencies looked at it [AAA is the top rating for an almost bullet-proof issue], yet it has the same yield differential over government bonds as a riskier BBB- or A-rated bond,' Platt explains. 'The last time I traded the F&C bond it was paying 1.2% more interest than government bonds [the safest of all]. Now, that might not sound like very much, but it is 0.5% above what I would get if I bought an equivalent rated bond in the marketplace.'

Platt also likes to favour issuers such as building group Taylor Woodrow, which issues both secured and unsecured bonds. Contrary to what you might think, the secured bond pays a higher yield to investors than the unsecured one.

Let's run that one again. These are examples of very safe bonds paying a yield associated with a rather riskier issue that has to be priced in such a way as to compensate investors for higher risk. You might say that something is wrong with this picture. After all, if, in the real world, your bank manager advanced a loan that was secured against your house, he would charge a lower rate of interest and so earn less profit. In Platt's corner of the bond world, things are upside down.

If you subscribe to the theory that markets are fully efficient then more people – the consensus, if you like – should be buying bonds like F&C, raising the price, reducing the yield and negating Platt's advantage. The reason that they don't, according to Platt, is that these secured bonds do not trade in large volumes and many bond managers are scared into the arms of the rated sector where liquidity is much greater. But, as Platt argues, liquidity often vanishes when you need it most – in this case, when you need to get rid of your bonds. 'What people tend to forget is that in times of need and trouble the investment banks may not be there to buy your bonds,' he says.

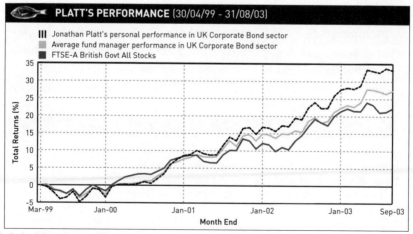

PLATT'S PERFORMANCE (30/04/99 - 31/08/03)

||| Jonathan Platt's personal performance in UK Corporate Bond sector
▓ Average fund manager performance in UK Corporate Bond sector
■ FTSE-A British Govt All Stocks

Total Returns (%) — *Month End*

* For further information see p192

Source: Citywire

This is one crucial difference among many between investing in equities and bonds. 'The equity markets are really much more sophisticated, with great liquidity and transparency. They are highly regulated, with market makers forced to trade at prices they quote on their dealing screens. That is not the case with corporate bonds. With bonds, trading is done over the counter – there is no central market and there is no guarantee of prices. So, while I can readily understand the need for liquidity, you don't need too much of it, especially if you are investing for the longer term. If you are doing that properly then you really should be emphasising the need for security in your portfolio.'

Talking of shares, there is a good deal of debate these days over how bond and equities fund managers and analysts within the same house can work together and help each other. Platt has a good perspective on the different approaches, having spent the first three years of his working life as an equities manager at Royal London. The approaches, he says, are very different. 'In a bond world you are interested as a manager in what can go wrong and that affects your mind-set. Another difference is that you don't have to be benchmark-oriented. In equities, managers, albeit not the best ones, have become fixated with benchmarks. I can pick up almost any general equity portfolio and be confident that I can name seven out of the 10 top holdings.'

Of course, one failure can have a much more dramatic effect on a bond portfolio than it can on an equities portfolio. 'If a stock underlying one bond goes bad it can undo not just one year's performance but multiple years. So that's why bond managers tend to be more pessimistic, more cynical and more sceptical about the growing emphasis on shareholder returns in the corporate sector over recent years.'

When it comes to choosing bonds, Platt works very closely with

---

CAREER PROFILE

1985-present: Platt has his professional roots firmly embedded in the Royal London culture, having been with the group for nearly 20 years. He became Head of Fixed Interest in 1992, and currently runs a broad range of portfolios including the Royal London Income fund, in which he has money invested in ISAs.

Eric Holt, his head of credit research at Royal London who has a similar background in choosing issues for life funds. Together they have come up with an internal rating system that picks up where the established agencies leave off, rating bonds not just for their probability of default but for their likely recovery rate should their issuers get into trouble.

Eschewing the letters system of the agencies, the Royal London system rates bonds between 1 (equivalent to a AAA rating) and 10 (the same quality as BBB-). Their rating system requires Platt's team to pore over the covenants of any secured bonds they might invest in and compare them with rated bonds. There is more than enough work to do as the corporate bond market has expanded rapidly in recent years. Issues become ever more complex in their terms, with companies slicing and dicing their businesses and issuing bonds to offer investors a chance to participate in the income streams they throw off.

Platt is proud of the work his team does and the intellectual property that works its way into his funds' performance, but he has no desire to set up in competition with the established credit-rating agencies. 'We don't do it as well as they do – they have greater access to management accounts and to the managers themselves than we do,' he says. 'In any case, we do a different job – we assess value, they gauge the probability of default.'

The agencies are often controversial bodies, especially with companies whose bonds they have downgraded, but Platt thinks they deserve a better image than the one they have. 'They are a strange kind of intermediary, which doesn't really exist in the equity markets. Generally they do work in an efficient manner, helping to disseminate information to the market.'

INVESTMENT STYLE

Platt calls himself a conservative investor but is really a radical at heart. He avoids the consensus of bond managers who stick with issues rated by the credit agencies. Instead he has found his niche by diverting part of his portfolio to higher-yield unrated bonds that are secured against a borrower's assets.

So does all the analysis at Royal London pay off? Platt is fairly sure it does. 'Over the last two to three years our exposure to bonds that have defaulted has been pretty low. We had no exposure to either WorldCom or Enron when they fell or crashed completely. I like to think that was a result of our intellectual process.'

The investment process aside, Platt is sure that his asset allocation process has a built-in safeguard that avoids the temptation to head for the more dangerous side of the street. 'If you have 20-30% of your bonds with greater security then you don't have to chase the riskier end of the market.'

All professional money managers are, to a greater or lesser extent, a product of the time they joined the markets and of the culture. That particularly applies to Platt who started his career in the mid-1980s by investing life assurance money. Times have moved on. 'It always comes back to the mentality of the team, and with us that very much reflects our background in investing in secured assets,' he says. 'People coming into the market now are being schooled very differently, with the emphasis on ratings. If you talk to many investors now they are very nervous about non-rated bonds and equate them with junk bonds.'

Platt is very keen to emphasise the importance of teamwork in Royal London and particularly his partnership with Eric Holt. Modesty forbids them from labelling their investment process the 'Platt-Holt' method and, as Platt admits, there was a certain amount of luck involved in his teaming up with Holt. 'We came together when Royal London took over United Insurance where Eric was working. We have very different personalities but he is even more of an advocate of this style than I am so his role is extremely important.'

The scope of the Royal London team has extended in recent years as the fixed-interest world has become more complex. Platt now works closely with Paul Doran, head of the group's quantitative team. 'Paul has a similar view to us on security and investment. As of now we do not do a huge amount of work with him, but it is increasing, especially in looking at the potential use of credit derivatives in our portfolios.'

Platt's early days in equity fund management also led him to recruit two equity analysts last year to play the role of what he describes as 'equity-style credit analysts'. He sees their background as bringing an extra dimension to the way he chooses bonds for investment. 'I think it would be fair to say that equity analysis has been superior to credit analysis,' says Platt. 'I believe that equity research is mostly deeper and better, with more emphasis on looking forward to events. By contrast, the perception of many credit analysts of how a company's credit rating may change has been too static.'

But Platt thinks there are limitations to what equity analysis can bring to his trade – a consequence, he acknowledges, of the two sides being rather different crafts. 'We share stuff across our Intranet site but co-operation can be difficult. It is important to get equity input but it would never be a determinant of what we invest in because bonds require a different type of analysis in the end.'

A relaxed and easy-going man, Platt is very much at ease with himself, the job he does at Royal London and the way he does it. While accustomed to finishing at or near the top of performance tables, he has no real curiosity about how rival managers go about their business. 'I don't have any wish to sound arrogant or insular, but if you believe in an investment approach, like I do, then I think it is very important to stick with it and not be blown off course.'

There are, he admits, a lot of good fixed-interest managers out there. 'I really don't know a great deal about how they do their jobs but that doesn't mean that there aren't some managers with great records on both the retail and institutional side.'

If you asked Platt what he particularly enjoys about his job he would probably give you two answers. The first would be that the team he runs is small enough to ensure that he can still get his hands dirty. 'The size of the team here is very deliberate – I want to make an impact in what I do and it allows me to continue to manage money as well as managing people.'

The second would be that he is able to return results that he says are 'not just good but consistent as well. I am very confident that whether we are presenting to our internal life funds, pension fund trustees or unit trust directors, we can be very consistent across the board.'

A History of Human Enterprise

D uring the prolonged bull market of the 1990s, and especially towards the end of it, a university debating society that tabled the motion 'Bonds are boring' would have found it hard to find any speakers to oppose. These were the glory dates of the stock-market – the cult of equities. Who needed interest rates of 4, 5 or even 6% a year when shares were doubling and trebling overnight and the Dow was inexorably heading for 36,000?

By their own admission, bond managers such as Jonathan Platt are on the lookout for bad news – what might make their investments crash and burn – and there wasn't an awful lot around as the bull market reached its crescendo. It was time for blue sky thinking. We all know what happened next. The stockmarket suffered its biggest ever destruction in value while bond managers, and those who had switched their pension funds from shares into bonds at the start of the new millennium, chuckled quietly to themselves and counted the money.

But there is a lot more to bonds than just a nice safeish sort of place to keep your money when the equity markets turn sour. In fact, far more so than shares, bonds tell the story of human enterprise and man's quest to change the world. Yes, equity markets have soared and dived, bringing tiny firms to industry dominance (think Vodafone) and consigning investors' pensions to the dustbin (think Enron). But bonds are much more than that. They have financed wars and, through the construction of railroads, opened up new empires. Time after time, the obligations to pay interest have simply been torn up by sovereign governments, sometimes because of ideological objections, sometimes because countries simply ran out of money. In short, bonds are the story of history itself. So, next time somebody tells you that bonds are boring, a sleep-inducing cocktail of credit ratings, yield curves and spreads, here is some counter-ammunition:

1. Bonds build and change the world. When it comes to globalisation, the bond markets were centuries ahead of equities. Back in the 14th Century England's King Edward I needed money to wage wars. He didn't waste his time underwriting a share issue – instead he issued bonds to the great Italian banking families of the time. Fast forward a few centuries and you find a group of Dutch families operating from The Hague buying bonds to finance the great coalition against Louis XIV led by William of Orange, while the pan-European Rothschild family network supported the British war effort against Napoleon.

But it was the railway mania of the second half of the 19th Century that established bonds as the primary, and often most infamous, form of capital project investment. Investors, almost entirely in Europe and mostly in London, wrote huge cheques to subscribe to bond issues that promised regular income streams as the railroad tracks rolled out from the established centres of the New World to the back of beyond. Some got their coupons paid, but many others could only hand down to their loved ones rather beautiful but worthless bond certificates that to this day adorn many a living room wall.

In many cases, ambition and blarney outstripped the business case for the railways. If the promised mineral riches of the mosquito-ridden interior turned out to be phoney, there was nothing to ship back and no revenue to pay the coupons.

One by one the markets went belly-up to the consternation of faraway investors. In 1873 the Northern Pacific Railroad in the US collapsed and about two-fifths of the country's railway bonds followed suit thereafter. It was Peru's turn in 1875, when the country's natural resources of guano ran out. Three years later it was Sweden's go – England started producing its own iron ore, killing Swedish exports and leaving the mine owners with nothing to pay the railroads with.

2. Bonds teach lessons that should be learned by any investor.
Everyone cheerfully compared the expansion of broadband telecommunications networks in the 1990s with the railroads of the 19th
Century – 'enterprise', 'vision' and 'new frontiers' were the buzz words
of the day. Of course, everybody forgot about the railroad bond
defaults that resulted from overcapacity and falling tariffs – until,
that is, it happened all over again. In 2002 Global Crossing, which
had laid 1.7 million miles of fibre-optic cable in a network connecting
27 countries, filed for bankruptcy with net debts of $10 billion,
financed in large part by bondholders.

3. Bonds cause people to say stupid things. Long before anybody
muttered anything about the Dow's inevitable progression to 36,000,
Citibank chief executive Walter Wriston said 'countries don't go bust'.
That was in the mid-1970s. Wriston and other bank chiefs took this
so much to heart that their banks issued bonds and loans to developing countries, mostly recycling the billions of petrodollars created my
the massive rise in oil prices after 1973. Wriston was wrong. Mexico
did go bust in 1982, defaulting on its loans and bonds. Brazil,
Argentina and a host of African nations followed suit, keeping the
IMF and World Bank busy ever since.

4. Bonds can bring out the worst in people. Was Michael Milken the
greatest bond market innovator of all time, or one of the industry's
biggest crooks? It was Milken who almost single-handedly invented
the junk-bond market in the 1980s, enabling companies and investors
with low credit status to raise huge sums of money by issuing high-
yield bonds.

The technique became hugely controversial as takeover merchants
asset-stripped companies to repay the interest on the bonds. It all
ended in tears. After making huge amounts of money for both himself
and his employers, Drexel Burnham Lambert, the US Justice
Department fingered Milken after arbitrageur Ivan Boesky implicat-
ed him in securities fraud. Milken was sentenced to 10 years in prison
and fined $1.1 billion after pleading guilty to six charges. He was
released after three years. Drexel filed for bankruptcy as the junk-
bond market crashed.

5. Bond gurus can have the same status as equity gurus. There may be fewer of them around but the top bond investors have an enormous following among the investing public. Probably the most famous of all is Bill Gross, dubbed 'The King of Bonds', who looks after $350 billion of fixed-interest investments as chief investment officer of US investment group Pimco.

The yoga-loving Gross, something of a new-age Californian, has beaten the market average for 23 out of the past 29 years and can turn a trading session around with a few well-chosen words on business television channels. His monthly market commentaries are eagerly awaited. They range from the sublime, with citations from Virginia Woolf and Alfred Lord Tennyson, to the faintly ridiculous – after the rapid stockmarket advance of mid-2003, Gross compared America's borrowing binge to the Newman family from the old *MAD* magazine (Motto: 'What, Me Worry?'). 'Are the Newmans worrying yet? Not if they bought stocks six months ago. Not if they refinanced their home in early June or bought that Hummer with 0% financing. But they will. The Newmans represent your future, your country and your money, and to think otherwise would clearly be MAD.'

6. Bond investors sometimes get the last laugh. It's no fun for any investor when a company falls on very hard times – shares plunge to near zero and bonds end up trading at just a few pence in the pound as interest payments are suspended. But if anyone has the chance to scrape a few ashes out of the fire it is usually the bondholders. Investors owning ordinary shares are bottom of the pile when it comes to recovering any assets.

When the hugely indebted British cable companies, Telewest and NTL found they couldn't pay their way in 2002, the bondholders ended up with near-total ownership of the assets. The ordinary shareholders ended up with a miserable 2% of a business they once owned all of.

David Winters
Distressed Debt

by Sunil Jagtiani

*O*n the face of it, a bankrupt company is an odd place to search
for a profitable investment opportunity. Think of the
scandalous, billion-dollar bankruptcies of energy trader
Enron and telecommunications specialist WorldCom, the biggest
collapses in US corporate history. The two firms declared bankruptcy
in 2001 and 2002 respectively, leading to huge losses for investors
amid allegations of fraud. Surely no sane investor would want to
invest in either firm once they hit trouble?

Distressed debt investors beg to differ. They are specialists who
invest in deeply troubled or bankrupt firms' corporate bonds, even
though the bonds have often defaulted on interest payments. They get
attracted when the price of a distressed or bankrupt firm's bonds plunges
as investors dump the security. Distressed debt investors aim to buy the
bonds at a knockdown price in the expectation that their true worth is
higher but obscured by mainstream investors' fear of owning a distressed
firm's securities. They anticipate making a profit once the firm has
returned to financial stability, revealing the true value of the bonds. The
US has the world's largest distressed debt market, and US fund manager
David Winters is one of the most experienced investors in the sector.

Winters' Wonderland

David Winters, President and Chief Investment Officer of Franklin Mutual Advisers, investment adviser to Mutual Series Fund Inc, took an interest in the stockmarket and bankrupt companies in his childhood. 'I've been interested in compounding capital since the age of five,' he says, 'and I was always interested in stocks and bankruptcies. Partly it was because I was surprised that there were people who had figured out how to make money during the US Great Depression between 1929 and 1941. But I also like railroads a lot, and bankruptcy is a big part of the history of railroad companies.' So, though Winters' early interest in bankruptcy is a little disconcerting, it is unsurprising that he ended up a specialist investor in troubled or bankrupt firms at Franklin Mutual Advisers. The firm, which manages about $26 billion worth of assets, is a subsidiary of California-based Franklin Resources, a company with a market value of $12 billion.

Winters became a fund manager when he graduated from college. His tenure at Franklin Mutual Advisers stretches back to 1987, when he joined a firm called Heine Securities, which subsequently became Franklin Mutual Advisers. 'I bought my first distressed bond at Franklin Mutual Advisers when I joined 16 years ago,' Winters says, 'and the company probably bought its first distressed bond in 1949, so we've been at this game a long time.' Apart from his role as the firm's president and chief investment officer, Winters heads up a group of fund managers and analysts colloquially named Team Distress. He oversees some $3.5 billion worth of assets invested in distressed corporate bonds. The assets are spread across a number of funds rather than concentrated in a single portfolio. Winters is lead or co-manager of most of those funds, including the $4.7 billion Mutual Beacon fund, which is open to US investors only, and other, smaller portfolios managed for European rather than US-based investors. Winters became co-manager of Mutual Beacon in 1998, since when the fund has risen by about 9%. This may look a modest gain, but it compares very favourably with the 22% slide over the same period in the key US S&P 500 index.

Franklin Mutual Advisers is known as a value investor in search of bargain-priced stocks. So as you might expect, Winters counts legendary value investors Benjamin Graham and Warren Buffett among his major influences. 'We have a big stake in Warren Buffett's Berkshire Hathaway, and I go to the Berkshire meeting every year,' he says. 'There's a lot to be learned from Warren. He has a lot of integrity. I've studied him, Graham and all the major value investors. I've also studied growth investors because there are different paths to investment nirvana. I don't think anybody has the absolute path to golden investment returns. It's very important to continue to have an open mind. You have to stay humble and you have to learn every day. You never know who you'll meet or what'll you learn.'

Winters feels the philosophy of value investing applies to distressed debt in a similar way that it applies to equities, in the sense that the overarching aim is to find securities trading at attractive or, even better, bargain prices. The key difference is that a distressed debt investor like Winters buys a troubled or bankrupt company's bonds, which count as part of the firm's debt, while those buying

DAVID WINTERS: THE MAN

David Winters was born in 1962. He graduated with a BA in Economics from Cornell University in 1984. He enjoys outdoor activities, trains and reading annual reports.

shares purchase a company's equity rather than its debt. Of course, equity investing is a much more popular and mainstream activity than distressed debt investing. Healthy corporate bonds also attract many more investors than distressed bonds. This is down to the fact that distressed debt investing is viewed as difficult and risky. Nevertheless, distressed debt specialists feel their sector offers rich rewards despite its lack of popularity.

The process of working out whether a distressed bond is worth buying is complex, but generally involves the following steps. You begin by working out what the troubled or bankrupt company's assets are worth. Then you work out how much a firm's creditors are owed and the priority of their claims. The latter is laid down in law although subject to the general contentious bankruptcy reorganisation process where creditors vie for the best treatment of their claims. The capital structure of the debt must be carefully analysed. The claims against the capital structure especially those in dispute must be analysed to try to determine the extent of their validity. For example, secured lenders like banks typically have first claim ahead of bondholders. But bondholders in turn take priority over shareholders. After doing this you can compare the claims with the firm's assets. This process will give you an estimate as to how much of the assets bondholders can lay claim to. This, in turn, tells you roughly what each bond is actually worth, or, to put another way, gives you the bond's underlying asset value. An investment opportunity can arise if the price the bond is trading at is below its underlying asset value. Note that under US law a distressed debt investor can buy a firm's bonds even if the business is bankrupt.

'You're really trying to determine what the estate in bankruptcy is worth,' Winters says. 'You work out the priority of the claims to determine a range of values for the bonds, and then see what kind of discount to those values the bonds trade at. What you want is plenty of upside and little downside. It's all about separating the negative emotion surrounding a bankrupt firm from its underlying asset value. In that sense, temperament is a major component of being a success-ful distressed debt investor, together with being rational and doing the work of analysing a company's assets and liabilities.'

Selecting a distressed bond, however, is not simply a matter of crunching numbers. A great deal of judgement is involved in estimating the value of a company's assets. Winters analyses the industry a firm operates in, examines its management team and uses different valuation measures in a bid to inform those estimates. 'There is no golden analytic bullet when it comes to valuation,' Winters says. 'We ask questions about the underlying economics of a business. Also we really pay attention to management teams and to what motivates them. Judgement is a critical element. I once asked retired US general Hal Moore about judgement. Moore wrote *We Were Soldiers Once... And Young*, which was made into the film *We Were Soldiers*, starring Mel Gibson as Moore's character. I asked, "How do you teach good judgement sir?" He said, "You can't, next question." So it's not so easy. It's about learning from your mistakes – making a mistake is bad, but making the same mistake twice is inexcusable – working hard and realising that things change.'

Once a distressed debt investor has bought a distressed bond, he has to wait for its issuer to return to financial stability to make his profit. If the firm has declared bankruptcy, he has to wait for it to emerge from bankruptcy. In the US a bankrupt firm often opts for Chapter 11 bankruptcy protection, a legal process that protects it from creditors to allow it to carry on trading. It is an option that gives the firm time to restructure, which is thought to be in the interests of both its employees and its investors. When the firm emerges from bankruptcy its debt is reorganised. Its old bonds are cancelled and a package of new bonds and shares is issued depending on the form of

---

◄ CAREER PROFILE

- 1985-87: KMS Investment Advisors.
- 1987: Heine Securities. In 1996 the company was taken over by Franklin Resources. Winters then became Director of Research in 2000. In 2001 he became Chief Investment Officer, and in 2002 he became Chairman and Chief Executive Officer. Winters runs a number of funds, including the Franklin Mutual Beacon fund, which has helped make his name.

the plan of reorganisation. If the distressed debt investor has got his sums right, the package should reflect the underlying asset value of the old bonds and so be worth more than the price he paid for them. 'The time frame for a firm to emerge from bankruptcy varies with each situation,' Winters says. 'It can be quite short, but generally a bankruptcy takes a couple of years to see its way through. That's when we get the value back. The debt gets refinanced, we get new securities and generally we're gone – we sell. Sometimes the shares in the restructured company can be attractive, so we might keep the package of newly issued debt and equity.'

Explained this way the process of distressed investing may sound simple. But the reality is somewhat different as there are many pitfalls to avoid. For example, the bankruptcy process could reveal a company has published improper accounts or traded fraudulently, which can make the most careful prior calculations of the firm's assets and liabilities redundant. 'The underlying quality of a business can deteriorate for many other reasons, which can hit the firm's asset value,' Winters says. 'Or it may be that the extent of the firm's liabilities had not been properly quantified. You don't want to see the liabilities side of the business growing. The other thing I've learned is that the legal process in the US can go all kinds of wild ways. We've tried to learn from that. Making a good decision about a bond in respect of these matters is partly down to experience. Some of it is art rather than science – it isn't purely a numbers game. We also monitor a firm very carefully by talking to its managers and competitors, and by keeping a close eye on the relevant industry.'

One example of an investment Winters took a hit on involved cable television company Adelphia Communications, whose woes led to one of the largest bankruptcies in US corporate history. The company had assets of $22 billion when it filed for Chapter 11 pro-

---

◆ INVESTMENT STYLE

Winters is a value investor in search of distressed or bankrupt firms' bonds trading at knockdown prices whose true worth is higher.

tection in June 2002. Adelphia was set up in 1972 by John Rigas and went on to become one of America's largest cable operators. However, during the first few months of 2002 it was hit by allegations of accounting irregularities and fraud. The scandal led the Rigas family to relinquish control of the firm, which had defaulted on some £7 billion worth of debt by the time it filed for bankruptcy protection. Many distressed debt investors cast an eye over the firm when it hit trouble, including Winters and his team at Franklin Mutual Advisers. 'We bought into Adelphia,' he says, 'but there were discrepancies in their accounts and the bonds we bought plunged in value. When the dust cleared we acquired some higher quality Adelphia bonds. The point is that when we make a mistake, we try to learn from it, often from problems emerges opportunity. We added to our Adelphia position at attractive levels which has been profitable at this point.'

Happily for him, Winters has many examples of profitable distressed debt investments, particularly among US utility companies. He cites Pacific Gas & Electric as a classic example of his investment style in action. The firm was California's largest utility company, providing power and natural gas to 13 million customers, when it filed for Chapter 11 bankruptcy protection in 2001. It hit the buffers because of a steep rise in wholesale power costs, which it was restricted from passing on to customers under legislation passed when the

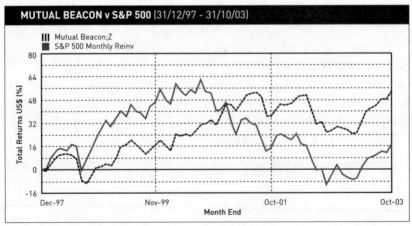

MUTUAL BEACON v S&P 500 (31/12/97 - 31/10/03)

||| Mutual Beacon;Z
■ S&P 500 Monthly Reinv

Total Returns US$ (%)

Month End

Source: Lipper

Californian energy market was deregulated in 1996. Pacific Gas & Electric's unreimbursed energy costs were running at more than $300 million per month and the firm had spent billions in excess of its revenues, in effect to subsidise power for its customers, by the time it filed for bankruptcy.

'Pacific Gas & Electric defaulted on its debt for a variety of reasons,' Winters says, 'though the rise in wholesale energy prices and deregulation were, of course, key. Its bonds slumped from 100 cents to the low 60s. We determined that the underlying asset value of the utility's plant and equipment covered those bonds at the least at 100 cents. So at 62 cents we felt that the bonds offered a low downside, big upside investment opportunity. California is the fifth or sixth largest economy in the world, and the likelihood that the energy industry would be reorganised was high, so we backed up the truck and bought a lot of bonds. In retrospect we should have bought more. Pacific Gas & Electric provides a basic product everybody needs. It was hit by the rise in wholesale energy prices, there were problematic regulatory issues, there were managerial issues, there were other structural issues, but ultimately those issues could be resolved through the bankruptcy process. So we figured when you bought the bonds at 60 cents, you set up an asset worth at least 100 cents. There was certainly ample asset cover to get your money back.'

Meanwhile, US electricity generator Calpine Corporation provides an example of a very troubled rather than bankrupt investment. During 2002 investors avoided the energy sector because of the collapse of companies such as Enron and Pacific Gas & Electric. This led to a major slide in Calpine's bond and share prices. 'Calpine used to be perceived as a growth stock, but its bond price declined to as low as 35 cents,' Winters says. 'We did our calculations and came to the conclusion that the value of the firm's plant and equipment covered the bonds at 70 cents. So we bought a lot of Calpine bonds in the summer of 2002, during the depths of despair. That has worked out well, and provides another example of separating the negative emotion surrounding a company from its underlying asset value.' In fact, the price of the Calpine bonds had more than doubled by the summer of 2003. 'This and the other examples help to illustrate that we are basically opportunistic value investors,' Winters adds. 'You know I don't think there are that many very serious value investors. It takes a certain sort of mental toughness to be a true value investor. This is because you have to go against the crowd whereas the urge to be with the herd is very, very strong.'

Nevertheless, talk of the big potential gains offered by the distressed debt sector may tempt investors to look at it seriously, even if it involves swimming against the tide. However, it is a specialist field of investment requiring a level of expertise few professional or private investors possess. In fact, many private investors know close to nothing about distressed debt and pay little attention to corporate bond prices generally. But Winters is keen to stress that investors who only put money into a firm's shares can still learn a lot from any bonds it has in issue. 'Sometimes the bond market is a lot smarter about equities than equity investors,' he says. 'So if you own stocks but you are a not a bond investor, you should still be paying attention to what the bonds are doing. If the bonds are struggling, you should take note. Remember, equities have a value because companies can meet their debt obligation. We view bonds and shares as forming a continuum of possible investment options.'

Part 2

Profiting from Bankruptcy

A well-worn piece of investment advice is to capitalise on poten-
tially profitable opportunities created during times of deep
pessimism, when the price of a security can tumble. Few asset
classes better exemplify this principle at work than the distressed
debt sector. The majority of private investors and most professional
fund managers want little to do with distressed corporate bonds,
which they view as very specialist and risky investments. After all, a
distressed bond has tumbled in value because of serious financial
problems at the firm that issued it. Very often the bond has defaulted
by failing to pay interest due to bondholders or because its issuer has
filed for bankruptcy. Conventional investors' understandable initial
reaction is to be fearful of distressed bonds in the light of these woes.
In contrast, the distressed debt specialist, occasionally and somewhat
unflatteringly referred to as a 'vulture' investor, sees an opportunity
amid all the fear. He wants to find a distressed bond trading at a
knockdown price whose true worth is higher but obscured by the fog
of negative sentiment created by its issuer's struggle for survival or
slide into bankruptcy.

A relatively small number of conventional mutual funds seek to invest
in distressed debt. David Winters himself describes distressed investing as 'an arcane back alley in the investment management industry',
likening it to a pond with big hungry fish (distressed companies) but

few fishermen (investors). The sector is better known for attracting the interest of so-called alternative investors, particularly hedge funds, which are complex investment vehicles aimed at sophisticated rather than mainstream investors. Nevertheless, the distressed debt sector is a substantial asset class. According to academic Edward Altman, a professor at New York University's Stern School of Business, the market value of publicly traded defaulted and distressed bonds reached $139.9 billion in 2002. Some $37.5 billion of this figure was accounted for by defaulted bonds (bonds that failed to make interest payments, or bonds issued by firms that have filed for bankruptcy), while the remainder, $102.4 billion, comprised distressed bonds. Altman's research also suggested that in 2002 some 21% of the market for lower-quality corporate bonds comprised distressed and defaulted bonds.

The professor distinguishes three investment styles in the distressed debt sector. One approach involves buying heavily into a firm's distressed bonds and eventually taking control of the failing business by swapping the bonds for shares. The investor, or group of investors, restructures the firm, runs it and restores it to health. The aim is to sell the shares after two to three years for a significant gain of between 20-25% over the price paid for the bonds. The second approach is to buy a firm's distressed debt and take an active part in influencing the way the business is restructured in bankruptcy. Unlike the first approach, investors do not seek to take control of, or run, the firm. They will get new bonds or a mixture of new shares, bonds and cash once the restructuring process is completed and the firm emerges from bankruptcy. They will then sell the securities, hoping for a handsome return over the price paid for the distressed bonds one or two years earlier. The last approach is simply to trade distressed securities over shorter time periods in the hope of turning a relatively quick profit of up to 20% rather than waiting to achieve a return after a restructuring process.

The second approach to distressed investing is the type practised by David Winters and many others. The US provides a key example of this kind of distressed debt investing at work because of the country's well-worked out bankruptcy laws, especially Chapter 11 of its bankruptcy code. Chapter 11 was passed into law in 1978 and is designed to give bankrupt businesses a degree of protection from creditors and bondholders while they reorganise in a bid to return to profitability and health. A firm carries on trading after filing for Chapter 11 but all major management decisions have to be ratified by the bankruptcy court. A reorganisation plan is worked out, which has to be accepted by creditors, bondholders and shareholders. The plan must treat creditors, bondholders and shareholders fairly and be approved by the bankruptcy court. If a company successfully emerges from bankruptcy, its prior debt obligations are cancelled and the debt is reorganised. Under this process bondholders will receive new bonds, or a mix of new bonds and shares, and sometimes cash, too. In the worst case scenario, a firm may fail to emerge from Chapter 11 bankruptcy, in which case it may liquidate. Alternatively, a firm may be in such dire straits that it opts for liquidation under Chapter 7 of the bankruptcy code rather than Chapter 11 when it first declares bankruptcy. But even when a firm is to liquidate, the distressed debt investor may have calculated that the business has sufficient assets to enable him to profit from buying its bonds.

Many large, high-profile US firms have filed for Chapter 11 bankruptcy protection recently, attracting vulture investors along the way. In 2002 alone US companies with assets worth a record $380 billion declared bankruptcy, according to research by BankruptcyData.com, up from $260 billion in 2001. Both years saw examples of the largest bankruptcies in US corporate history. First came energy company Enron's $63 billion bankruptcy at the end of 2001, at the time the largest ever. Then, in 2002, telecommunications specialist WorldCom's $107 billion collapse eclipsed Enron's to become the biggest in history. Other major US bankruptcies in 2002 included telecommunications firm Global Crossing, United Airline's parent firm UAL, Adelphia Communications and giant retailer Kmart, one of America's best-known chains of stores. A number of these bankruptcies involved accounting irregularities, allegations of fraud and massive investor losses, but many vulture investors picked over the firms' carcasses to search for profitable opportunities.

There were a number of triggers for the spate of bankruptcies that occurred after the turn of the millennium, but the stockmarket collapse that began in 2000 together with the economic downturn that followed were among the key factors. This helps to illustrate that investment activity levels in the distressed debt sector vary with the economic cycle. In good times fewer firms go bust, but in an economic downturn even big companies can hit the wall. Another important attribute of the distressed debt sector, according to research by Professor Altman, is that its performance bears little correlation with other asset classes, in particular the equity market. For example, his Altman-NYU Salomon Center Defaulted Bond index, which measures the performance of defaulted bonds, rose 11% in 1999, fell 33% in 2000, rose 17% in 2001, then slipped back 6% in 2002. In contrast, the US S&P 500 index performed very differently during the same years. In 1999 it rose by 21%, fell 9% in 2000, fell 12% in 2001 and then fell 22% in 2002.

Some professional investors commit a proportion of the assets they run to distressed debt because the sector performs in a different way to equities. They view the strategy as a way to diversify their investments to deal with the risk that equities can fall in value. Nevertheless, it must be stressed that distressed debt itself is a very risky asset class best suited to expert investors. Some expert or well-advised private investors might want to commit a small proportion of their cash to the distressed debt sector to further diversify their investment portfolios. Even so, the principle of *caveat emptor*, or buyer beware, most certainly applies.

The Ascent of Man

by Richard Lander

*H*edge funds are an increasingly important part of the investment scene, and one of the most common ways they are
distributed is as fund of hedge funds packages. Investment
professionals such as David Huyton, Nick Cavalla and Michael
Lozowski of Man Group spend much of their time selecting the funds,
many of them specialist and esoteric, that get combined into these
packages. Sales of Man's structured products, which come with a
capital guarantee, have soared in recent years as investors' knowledge
of hedge funds and their capabilities has risen sharply. In the future
more and more 'ordinary' investors are likely to consider hedge fund
products for their portfolios.

Picking Hedge Fund Managers

The world of hedge funds, or alternative investments, is charac-
terised by a preponderance of small players. The funds
themselves are run by small teams – perhaps just one or two
managers – and the outfits that package and distribute them are often
built on a small scale, too.

The very location of London's hedge fund industry is telling. While
the bulk of conventional, or long-only, fund managers and their sales
and distribution machines are in the skyscrapers and massive open-
plan floors of the Square Mile, their counterparts in the hedge fund
world are clustered around the dignified thoroughfares of St James in
the heart of the West End. Pick any elegant Georgian townhouse
around Duke Street, complete with discreet brass plate and heavy
door knocker, and you are likely to find a hedge fund related business
behind it.

Against this background of small organisations, Man Group stands
out prominently. From its 18th Century roots as a trader on the
London soft commodities markets – its home is still in Sugar Quay by
the Thames – it is now the world's biggest player in hedge funds, or
alternative investments.

Under a variety of brand names developed through organic growth
and acquisition, Man Investments, the asset management division,
now has more than $30 billion of funds under management. The Man
products are distributed through a global network of private banks,

investment advisers and other intermediaries to meet the growing appetite for hedge funds among institutional investors and the top strata of wealthy individuals.

The appeal of Man's hedge fund products to these investors is obvious. Investing in a wide range of styles, many of the products are engineered to offer investors at least 100% of their money back when they mature. Man's capital guarantees are underwritten by leading banks, and actually work.

Of course, the whole point of hedge fund products is that they do rather better than that. Through a variety of investment styles these funds can reach areas that are way beyond the remit of conventional funds. If a hedge fund manager doesn't like a share, he or she can 'short' it (sell it with the hope of buying it back at a lower price later). Other hedge funds invest in derivatives on stocks, bonds and interest rates so that the profit effect of getting a bet right is considerably enhanced. With a few strict exceptions, long-only fund managers can't do that.

A well-accepted definition of a hedge fund demonstrates just how wide their scope is: '*It is a fund that can take both long and short positions, use arbitrage, buy and sell misvalued securities, trade options or bonds, and invest in almost any opportunity in any market where it foresees impressive gains at reduced risk.*'

The ultimate aim of any hedge fund strategy is to make money across a complete range of market scenarios, including many where conventional investment routes make that almost impossible, so that the capital return guarantee isn't needed.

Here again, Man has walked the walk. As an example, Man-IP 220 Ltd has shown an annualised return of 18.9% since inception on 18 December 1996 to 30 September 2003, while the FTSE 100 index rose by just 1.8% over that whole period.

So the job of the senior executives at Man Investments is somewhat different from the other managers in this book. Their responsibility is not to choose the right stocks for one or more funds but to choose the right *managers* across the gamut of alternative investment styles. The ultimate aim – happy investors enjoying market-leading returns – is, of course, similar in all cases.

In recognition of this, Man puts considerable resources into manager selection at its wholly owned investment managers: AHL; Glenwood; RMF; and, particularly, Man Global Strategies. With a manager selection and oversight team of 14, this division has increased its number of managers from five to 30 over the past five years, while funds under management have soared fivefold to $5 billion.

The manager selection at Man Global Strategies is overseen by Man's chief investment officer, David Huyton, his co-head of investment management, Mike Lozowski, and global head of manager selection, Nick Cavalla.

As a hedge fund manager, getting on the Man Global Strategies roster is not easy. As a very big hitter in the hedge and alternative strategies world, Man can tap a wide variety of sources to be sure it hears about any manager worth knowing. These sources range from personal contacts, prime brokers and industry conferences to headhunters, corporate financiers with businesses for sale, and direct approaches from managers themselves.

In any given year the Man team might talk to as many as 700 managers. A lot of these enquiries will be at a very preliminary level. Huyton and his team then get into some heavy-duty filtering. In terms of really serious conversations – where Man does detailed due diligence on a potential manager – about 50 will be considered, of which perhaps 15 will make it into the active ranks of Man managers.

Alternative investing may involve sophisticated techniques but the first filter in choosing a manager is as straightforward as they come – their track record. 'They have got to show some consistent

---

CAREER PROFILE: DAVID HUYTON

David Huyton is the CIO and a director at Man Investments with responsibility for research and the management of in-house funds. He joined AHL in 1987, focusing on quantitative trading methods. He has an Honours degree in Physics and Theoretical Physics from Cambridge University and a Masters in Applied Statistics and Operational Research from the University of London.

alpha,' says Mike Lozowski. 'The first pre-requisite is some evidence that a manager can deliver returns that are not predominantly beta to the market.'

Perhaps more surprising is David Huyton's assertion that it may be better to get involved with an alternative strategy manager at an early stage rather than when they have several years of experience (and hence a longer track record) under their belt. Not only is that counter-intuitive, it is also contrary to what most fund of funds managers in the conventional investing arena would say. Not for the first time, things are different in the world of alternatives.

'It is difficult to get hard research in a deep way because of the nature of these things, but there is some evidence that managers perform better in their early stages,' says Huyton. 'At the same time, by getting in early you can very often get a better deal and fashion the products according to your own taste.'

But, as Nick Cavalla points out, one does have to be careful about making too many generalisations, particularly when a traditional long-only fund manager is making a first leap into alternatives. 'Do that and to a certain extent you are making a leap of faith,' he says. 'However, there is evidence that more established managers do tend to lose focus. Perhaps they get wealthy [successful alternative fund managers can generate enviable performance fees] and bored and end up running things to preserve their business rather than to preserve returns.'

Cavalla thinks early-stage managers have a greater 'degree of focus', and one of the aims that Man has when it gets involved with a new manager is to help them keep that. That means letting them manage money and get on with the job they are good at rather than getting bogged down in administration and marketing, functions that Man can do better from its own larger resources.

Having looked at the manager's overall credentials from 30,000 feet, Huyton and his team also drill down closely to examine the nuts and bolts of how he or she goes about their business. A decent track record is fine but, more importantly, was it achieved through skill or just good luck? The Man team carries out detailed statistical analysis to

determine the reason for a manager's success, concentrating, in particular, on whether the track record rests on just a few key decisions.

On top of that, Huyton wants to be convinced that managers know
the reasons for his own success. 'Managers need to articulate their
unique selling point to us while we have to connect that with their
past lives. We do that by checking out how they did in the market and
consulting references so we can see the pedigree of where they are
coming from.'

Away from the purely numerical, Cavalla feels it is important to
know all about a manager's investment process. 'We look at this in
some detail – at how it's constructed, what their information sources
are, their research process and their risk management techniques.
We'll take a snapshot of their portfolio and ask them to explain why
they have those positions. The snapshot needs to be aligned closely
with the rationale. If not, we would take that as a warning signal.'

One issue that Cavalla is keen to work through with his fund
managers is the question of risk management, as he sometimes
encounters the classic case of the tail wagging the dog. 'Managers
know that people want very low downside risk so they then take it
upon themselves to explain in huge detail about how they are not
going to lose money for clients. So what you end up with is one page
of how they are going to make strong alpha returns and 15 pages
about their risk-management techniques. That is completely the
wrong way around in my opinion,' says Cavalla. 'Of course risk management is relevant but it is, in fact, far better to have superior alpha
and adequate risk management than the other way round.'

Risk is part of the alternative investment strategies game, he
argues. 'You have to take a certain amount of risk. If you eliminate it
all you end up investing in a Treasury Bill. We have a capital return
guarantee on our products and we have found that if you have a floor
like this on your losses then investors are less worried about volatility.
One of our problems is getting our managers to take *more* risk
because we can handle the risk ourselves at the higher product level.'

Another criterion for Huyton – and generally an issue of high
importance throughout the hedge fund and alternative investment

world – is that of capacity. You might discover the greatest manager in the world for a particular investment strategy but then find that his or her way of investing makes it only workable with a very small level of funds. As in conventional investing, some approaches to the market simply don't work above a certain level of money. In this regard, Huyton has the interests of his colleagues close to his heart when looking for potential managers.

'We have to justify a manager's capacity capabilities for our retail network and for our fixed overheads,' he says. 'We have to ask ourselves, "Can we get sufficient funds with this or that manager if we find that he works well for us? Can he take $100 million or $200 million from us?" If he can only take a small amount then it really does become a huge administrative burden for us.'

To mitigate this, Man takes certain steps to have the right claims to a manager's capacity. In some cases, it acts as the exclusive distributor for the manager. In others, it has arrangements for a defined percentage of capacity that can be filled up over time if the relationship is seen to be working well.

While the recruitment process into the Man family is rigorous, inclusion can often lead to spectacular growth for the chosen managers. One example is Marin Capital Partners, a convertible bond arbitrage manager based in California. After meeting up with Man in 1998, following a lead from the prime brokerage community, the two sides negotiated a joint venture that took four months to bolt down before Marin could start managing money on Man's behalf in 1999.

CAREER PROFILE: NICK CAVALLA

Nick Cavalla is Head of Manager Selection within Man Global Strategies and Associate Director of Man Investments Ltd. He leads the discovery and due diligence process underpinning the numerous strategic investment relationships Man Global Strategies shares with its associated managers. Prior to joining Man Investments, he was a director of GNI Ltd, where he managed capital in foreign exchange and fixed-income markets as a Commodity Trading Adviser. Other former employers include NatWest Investment Management and Touche Ross Management Consultants. He holds an MA in Mathematics from Cambridge University

As Lozowski says, it was a good time to start trading after the trauma suffered by the capital markets in the wake of the collapse of the Long Term Capital Management (LTCM) hedge fund in late 1998, an event that shattered the confidence of the industry and sent shock-waves through the world's entire financial system. 'We put in the first $25 million to Marin. Now its capacity is $2 billion, of which about 50% is ours.'

As a behemoth in the field, with huge marketing capabilities, Man has a lot to offer relatively small managers. 'One strength is that we are a very stable source of capital for these managers and that is a very attractive feature. The last thing that any of them wants is large swings in their funding base, especially if they trade illiquid instruments, as many of them do. A lot of managers worked at businesses that were very badly shaken by the LTCM collapse.'

Man also offers a concept in London called the 'trader hotel' to help promising managers concentrate on running their business. While the room service may not be five-star, Man's hotel concept allows traders to prove their worth under Man's noses, while administrative affairs are taken care of. One manager who benefited from the hotel scheme was New York-based fixed-income arbitrageur Bob Treue. Having traded on his own account for a year, Treue bought his track record to Man. Duly impressed, Man drip-fed Treue with small amounts of its own money before entrusting him with client money. With things going well, Treue checked into the trader hotel for six months so that Man could monitor his progress further and get the due diligence process under way. In three years Treue's business has gone from virtually nothing to $500 million, with Man providing 90% of the funds.

CAREER PROFILE: MICHAEL LOZOWSKI

Michael Lozowski is Co-head of Man Global Strategies and a director of Man Investments Ltd. Prior to his current role he was Corporate Finance Director at Man Investments from 1990-1995. He joined Man Group in 1987 as Assistant Treasurer He holds a Masters degree in Physics from Oxford University and an MSc in Operational Research from the University of Sussex..

Once inside the Man family, managers and their performance are continually monitored. There is an initial six-month probationary period but Huyton is at pains to stress that there is no life-or-death decision at the end of that period. 'We have realistic expectations of what managers can achieve. Others might rush in, then find the manager has a bad six months and pull out again. But we have our own belief of what a manager can deliver.

'If performance really goes outside acceptable boundaries then we might decrease risk or reduce our allocation. But we are reasonably patient investors and we tend to stick with things until we are persuaded otherwise.'

HEDGE FUNDS

Hedge funds exist in a variety of styles. Here are some of the most commonly used:

Arbitrage: A two-sided strategy involving the purchase and sale of related securities that are mispriced compared with each other. Different strategies can focus on equities, convertible securities and debt instruments.

Directional: Based upon speculation of market direction in multiple asset classes, including currency exchange rates, interest rates and commodities.

Equity Market Neutral: A portfolio construction balanced between long positions in undervalued equities and short positions in overvalued equities. Returns come from out-performance of the long portfolio in rising markets and out-performance of the short portfolio in declining markets.

Long/Short Equity: This strategy goes long and short in equities. Returns are generated from long positions, short positions, gross exposure and cash.

Managed Futures: Leveraged, directional trading in currency, financial and commodity futures using quantitative models.

Global Macro: This strategy involves making leveraged, directional, opportunistic investing in global currency, equity, bond and commodity markets on a discretionary basis. Managers use a top-down global approach with trading views based on fundamental economic, political and market factors.

Market timing: A strategy that involves trying to enter and exit the markets at the right time. Managers switch between different markets and securities.

A completely different world it may be but, as was noted in the beginning of this chapter, the aims of a hedge fund selector such as Huyton and any of the other leading conventional managers in this book are remarkably similar in the end. And, while every manager will eventually give up on a share that fails to perform, so the Man team will end a relationship with a manager.

'There will always be some turnover of managers,' says Huyton. 'You have to accept that not everything always works out as it is supposed to do'.

Part 2

Here to Stay and Getting Bigger

T he old adage proclaims that you should be careful what you wish for because it might just happen. In the hedge fund industry it is a saying that rings true. Having enjoyed phenomenal growth over the last decade, all managers, distributors and fund of funds marketers would like and expect growth to continue and even to accelerate. It is just that all concerned would like it to happen in an orderly fashion.

Twelve years ago there were just a few hundred hedge funds, mostly located in the US, running about $100 billion under management. By the end of 2002 those figures had ballooned to 5000 funds running about $600 billion of assets. The variety of funds is now remarkable, with pretty well every strategy, asset class and geographical area now covered in some depth. That represents growth of about 20% a year over a period that encompassed one of the most remarkable equity bubble of all time followed by an equally amazing destruction of investor value as the world's stockmarkets descended into freefall after the first quarter of 2000.

But we have scarcely even begun. At the end of last year the world's liquid financial assets were estimated at about $58,000 billion, split between bonds ($38,000 billion) and equities ($20,000 billion). In other words, scarcely 1% of these liquid assets are invested through hedge funds. The obvious conclusion is that there is still plenty of room for growth.

Even at this level, the acceptance of hedge funds is remarkably skewed among institutional investors. According to one industry expert, US pension funds allocate 3.5% of their assets to alternative strategies (including private equity). If that sounds modest, contrast it with the UK where the equivalent figure is 0.3%, or less than one-tenth of that figure. If this was the history of the development of heat and light, we are probably at the stage of cavemen gazing in wonder at the campfire.

The battle to get major institutions to follow the lead of wealthy individuals and the canniest asset managers into hedge funds has been hard. In essence, there has been both push and pull, with fear and suspicion on one side (aided and abetted by a few high-profile fund collapses and scandals) and, on the other, a realisation that some of the alternative strategies under the hedge fund banner must now occupy a place in asset allocation.

Ask a conservative pension fund trustee why he or she doesn't or won't consider using hedge funds and they will not be short of answers. The most common ones are:
* Hedge funds are illiquid both in the way they are traded and in terms of the instruments they often invest in.
* They are not transparent in the way that highly regulated conventional funds are.
* Their managers charge fees that are much higher than conventional funds.

Although these statements are all true, it can be argued that it is these very features that make hedge funds so successful. Regarding illiquidity, compared with conventional funds, most hedge funds are, indeed, illiquid. But that is one reason why many hedge funds have performed as well as they have done. Managers can pursue investment strategies without having to worry about sudden bouts of fund withdrawals that force funds to dump their underlying holdings at what might be the wrong time.

As far as transparency is concerned, transparency in hedge funds is lower than in the bulk of conventional funds because the intellectual property quotient is usually much higher. The bulk of long-only fund managers fight a desperate battle for competitive edge within the restraints of their mandate in a world where the information they use is often available to everyone. Hedge fund managers, by contrast, continually search for new information angles that they can keep to themselves and trade with to their advantage.

And as for fees, well, yes, headline-grabbing rates of 35% and more in the hedge fund world would make any guardian of money choke on their food. Yet the bulk of hedge fund fees are performance-related. This is a massive contrast to the conventional fund world, where the poorer fund managers can make a very nice living just by turning up at the office.

While institutions absorb the philosophical arguments for and against hedge funds, a more dramatic and real-life lesson has been played out in the equity markets. The wounding bear market of 2000-2003, coming in the wake of two decades of almost continuous progress in share prices, brought home some uncomfortable truths. Suddenly the guardians of pension fund money found out that most of the equity managers they were dealing with – passive index trackers and active managers alike – were losing them huge amounts of cash. The contrast with both hedge managers, who are able to adopt strategies that can benefit from falling markets, and the few long-only managers who managed to preserve clients' money in that time – opened many people's eyes.

So the likelihood now is that more money from all sources – asset managers, institutional funds and private investors – is likely to flow into hedge funds. But please, says the hedge fund industry, let it happen at a sensible rate. If the UK pension fund industry alone put just 3% of its assets into hedge funds, some £30 billion of orders would flow into the market. The industry's capacity would either burst (or be supplemented by some very low-quality interlopers) while the effect on many underlying instruments would be destabilising.

Glossary

Agency trade A deal to trade stocks through an intermediary such as a stockbroker.

Balance sheet A financial document stating a company's assets, liabilities and net worth at a particular time.

Bottom-up investing The technique of finding investments by analysing individual companies to see if their shares (or bonds) are attractively priced. The opposite to top-down investing.

Contrarian investor One who tends to buy a security when most investors are selling it, or to sell a security when most investors are buying it. A contrarian seeks to buy a security for a low price when it is unpopular, and to sell it for a higher price once its popularity has recovered.

Discounted cashflow valuation A way of calculating the present value of a company's shares based on estimates of how much money it will have in the future once the costs of its operations have been taken into account.

Dividend Money a firm pays to its shareholders out of earnings. Usually expressed as a dividend per share and usually paid regularly (for example, every six months).

Dividend income Earnings funded by dividends.

Dividend yield The dividend per share expressed as a percentage of the share price.

Earnings per share A company's earnings divided by the number of shares it has in issue. Commonly shortened to 'EPS'.

Enterprise value The sum of a company's debt plus its market capitalisation. Best thought of as the cost of acquiring a company, which involves buying its shares and taking on its debt.

Fair value Describes a share (or bond) that is neither expensive nor cheap.

Free cashflow The amount of money a firm has once you subtract the costs of its operations.

Intrinsic (business) value The true value of a firm, often calculated by estimating how much money it will have left in the future once you subtract the costs of its operations.

Junk, or high-yield, bonds Risky bonds issued by firms. Junk bonds pay a high rate of interest, hence the term 'high yield', but carry a greater risk of default.

Long position Where an investor buys a stock, bond, currency or other instrument and hopes to make money when the value of that instrument rises.

Market capitalisation A company's price per share multiplied by the number of shares the company has in issue.

Market neutral A style of investing where a manager derives returns from balancing long and short positions in stocks or other instruments.

Mis-priced stock Used to describe a stock thought to be cheap or expensive, usually the former.

Net asset value A measure of a company's worth, calculated by subtracting its liabilities from its assets. Sometimes expressed as net asset value per share, which involves dividing a company's net asset value by the number of shares it has in issue.

PEG ratio A valuation measure used by growth-at-a-reasonable-price (Garp) investors. It divides a stock's price-to-earnings ratio by its percentage rate of annual earnings growth. Garp investors tend to prefer companies with PEG ratios below 1.

Price-to-book ratio A measure that compares a firm's stockmarket value with its assets. It is calculated by dividing the firm's share price by its net asset value per share.

Price-to-cashflow ratio A way of valuing a company. Calculated by dividing a firm's price per share by its cashflow per share.

Price-to-earnings, or P/E, ratio The best-known way of valuing a stock. It divides the price of a firm's share price by its earnings per share.

Programme trade A trade of a basket of stocks, often done automatically by computer according to a fund manager's prescribed quantitative instructions.

Reinvested dividends The process of buying more shares using dividends, or, put another way, of reinvesting dividends into the stockmarket.

Return-on-equity ratio A measure that compares a firm's profits with the capital provided by its shareholders.

Risk The possibility of an investment's expected return deviating from its actual return.

Short position - Where an investor sells borrowed securities in the hope of buying them back at a lower price in the future. Shorting is a way of making money from falling prices.

Technical analysis The discipline of using charts of a stockmarket's or share's past performance to predict future price movements. Technicians claim the charts reveal repeating patterns that can be used to make relatively accurate forecasts.

Top-down investing The technique of analysing broad economic, stockmarket and industrial trends to find stock investments. The opposite of bottom-up investing.

Valuation The process of determining if a security is cheap, fairly priced or dear.

Volatility The degree to which a security's price fluctuates. The more it fluctuates, the more volatile it is.

Yield The dividend paid by a share, or the interest paid by a bond, expressed as a percentage of the share or bond price.

Index

About Citywire

Citywire is an independent financial publishing group headquartered in London and 25 per cent owned by Reuters, the world-renowned news and information group. Founded in 1999, it has gained a strong reputation for both its innovative approach and professionalism.

Citywire has built a unique database which measures the performance of more than 3000 individual fund managers operating in 16 different countries in Europe and Asia. Citywire tracks the people, not the funds. It builds up a track record for each of manager as they move jobs or change responsibilities within the same company. The methodology is objective, independent and approved by external actuaries. Citywire ranks fund managers on their absolute performance and rates them according to their risk-adjusted returns.

All Citywire's editors and senior staff correspondents have passed appropriate regulatory exams set for financial advisers on funds and shares. Citywire itself has chosen to become a regulated entity coming under the jurisdiction of the UK's premier financial watchdog, The Financial Services Authority. Citywire's activities encompass: print publications; international fund manager performance data; events; online publishing; content syndication; and BrainsTrust data – exclusive information on the best investment ideas of the best managers.

If you would like a free copy of our corporate brochure email mhasson@citywire.co.uk or write to Marion Hasson, Production Director, Citywire Financial Publishers, 1st Floor, 87 Vauxhall Walk, London SE11 5HL.

For more information about Citywire and its publishing activities visit the 'About Us' section of the Citywire website – *www.citywire.co.uk*.